Also by Emily Crawford, Ph.D.

Crawford, Emily, Colleen F. Moore, and Valerie Ahl. 2004. "The roles of risk perception, borderline and antisocial personality characteristics in college alcohol use and abuse." *Journal of Applied Social Psychology* 34(7): 1371-1394.

Crawford, Emily, and Margaret O'Dougherty Wright. 2007. "The impact of childhood psychological maltreatment on interpersonal schemas and subsequent experiences of relationship aggression." *Journal of Emotional Abuse* 7(2): 93-116.

Crawford, Emily, Margaret O'Dougherty Wright, and Zachary Birchmeier. 2008. "Drug-facilitated sexual assault: College women's risk perception and behavioral choices." *Journal of American College Health* 57(3): 261-272.

Crawford, Emily, Margaret O'Dougherty Wright, and Ann Masten. 2005. "Spirituality and resilience in adolescents." In *Handbook of Spiritual Development in Childhood and Adolescence,* edited by Eugene C. Roehlkepartain, Pamela Ebstyne King, Linda M. Wagener, and Peter L. Benson, 355-370. Thousand Oaks, CA: Sage Publications.

Wright, Margaret O'Doughtery, Emily Crawford, and Darren Del Castillo. 2009. "Childhood emotional maltreatment and later adaptation: The mediating role of core relational schemas." *Journal of Child Abuse and Neglect* 33: 59-68.

Wright, Margaret O'Doughterty, Emily Crawford, and Katie Sebastian. 2007. "Positive resolution of childhood sexual abuse experiences." *Journal of Family Violence* 22(7): 597-608.

God
is
Talking

How a Green Iguana Taught Me to Listen

......

Emily Crawford, PhD

InspiringVoices®
A Service of **Guideposts**

Scriptures taken from the Holy Bible, New International Version®, NIV®. Copyright © 1973, 1978, 1984, 2011 by Biblica, Inc.™ Used by permission of Zondervan. All rights reserved worldwide. www.zondervan.com. The "NIV" and "New International Version" are trademarks registered in the United States Patent and Trademark Office by Biblica, Inc.™

Inspiring Voices books may be ordered through booksellers or by contacting:

Inspiring Voices
1663 Liberty Drive
Bloomington, IN 47403
www.inspiringvoices.com
1 (866) 697-5313

Because of the dynamic nature of the Internet, any web addresses or links contained in this book may have changed since publication and may no longer be valid. The views expressed in this work are solely those of the author and do not necessarily reflect the views of the publisher, and the publisher hereby disclaims any responsibility for them.

ISBN: 978-1-4624-0793-4 (sc)
ISBN: 978-1-4624-0794-1 (e)

Library of Congress Control Number: 2013919340

Printed in the United States of America.

Inspiring Voices rev. date: 11/6/2013

For my beloved green girl Sammy, and Zak, Iguana Papa

Contents

Preface

*I*f you have opened this book, then you are probably open to hearing about God. Have there been times in your life when you felt like God was silent? This book was written, in part, to address this phenomenon. Listening for God is like a muscle we have to exercise. If we do not ask, seek, and knock, God does not force His way in.[1] I am Christian, and I write from a Christian perspective. Friends of many different faiths and friends of no faith have also given positive feedback on my book, so I think you will find that you can connect with the journey even if you are approaching it from a different angle.

How does a green iguana named Sammy teach us to listen to God? Well, she teaches as a wild, petite but tough beloved green girlish rough scaly thing with a mysterious smile, made by a humorous and magnificently creative almighty one who I love more every day. Through Sammy, I have become more aware of God's presence as well as His nature. Loving, gentle, humorous, playful, joyous—did I mention loving? When God gave me a precious gift such as Sammy, I felt compelled to do more than just avoid taking her for granted. I decided to share the gift, which is why I wrote this book.

In the first chapter, "How It All Began," you will learn the uncanny timing of Sammy's entry into my life, which established her as a tiny but powerful symbol of hope in a hurting world. In "Let's Get Sambunctious," I joyfully reflect on my appreciation of God's humor in creating such a unique creature as the green iguana. After reading "Common Questions" about green iguanas that are highlighted throughout the book, learn

---

[1]   Matthew 7:7 (New International Version).

about what Sammy teaches us as an ambassador for a God of balance who wants us to be healthy and happy, in "Holistic Health." Then, read about "Why Sammy Is My Green Angel." You might also be surprised to learn just how attentive, sensitive, and emotionally expressive a nonverbal creature like Sammy is, in "Emotional Intelligence." Learning about the plethora of communication that occurs in the nonverbal realm has certainly made me better able to listen for God's still small voice.[2] God continued to use Sammy to assure me of His loving presence during the most difficult times in my life; read about this and more in "Seasons" and "Resilience." In "Mindfulness And Relaxation," Silent Sammy reminds us to slow down and listen for the presence of God. "Be silent before me . . ."[3] Finally, bask in reflection on lizard lessons in "Love."

While I consider my book to consist of very accurate information about how to best care for the green iguana, this book does not substitute for the stellar green iguana care manuals that already exist and which are referenced throughout my book. Instead, my words are a window into the life of one very special iguana, my baby girl Samantha. I also include her detailed care instructions in an appendix. Maybe you are curious about how a bond with such a unique animal could teach us life lessons in love, while simultaneously drawing us to a realization that there is a great loving interconnectedness among life. Maybe you really just want to know more about how someone could feel so strongly about a lizard! Either way, this book is for you, and I hope you enjoy it.

---

[2]   1 Kings 19:12.

[3]   Isaiah 41:1.

Baby Sammy shortly after adoption.

How It All Began

September 11, 2001. Madison, Wisconsin. I am running late as usual. I jump off the bus and practically skip into the psychiatric clinic where I have been working as a research assistant for the past year. This is my first job out of college, and I am planning to apply to graduate school in psychology. It is a beautiful fall day, and I feel refreshed from the crisp air and brisk walk. I push my blond hair out of my face and tuck it behind my black-rimmed glasses, adjust my red collared shirt, and settle into my small office. Then I make my good morning rounds. I see my coworker and give her a cheery "Good morning!" I have no idea what she means when she says, "You haven't heard," her voice flat, eyes large, and a worried crease on her forehead. *Why is she so serious?* I still do not even begin to grasp the gravity of the situation, even as she goes on about towers and planes and terrorism. It is only when she tearfully expresses her concern about her brother's whereabouts that reality begins to set in. Suddenly, everything slowly draws into focus. My cousin works at the Pentagon. Many of my coworkers have family they are trying to reach. Everything stops. And then we are all together, workers I have not yet met, united by a surreal moment suspended in time as we watch, from the safety of our lunchroom, the second tower collapse. I am struck by the varied reactions, from "See, now it's your turn America" to "No place is safe" to "What's the big deal?" Some are crying about the end of the world. That night, my boyfriend puts his feet up on the restaurant bench, smiling, mocking those whose shock lingers. He's in the "What's the big deal?" category. This moment marks the beginning of the end of our relationship.

Now, I wonder, was my Sammy born yet?

Everything remains in sharp focus. You know, those moments in time that are etched so clearly in the mind. Nothing is certain. It is with this mindset that I watch, weeks later, from my apartment on State Street. I watch the students loudly announcing their move from one bar to the next. I watch the homeless, the distressed, and the distraught. I watch the storekeepers competing for sales, constantly rearranging their outdoor clothing racks and marking down their prices. I open my windows and the scents of coffee, fried cheese curds, and beer drift into my studio apartment as the noise amplifies. There is someone picking at a guitar on the corner. A harmonica. A drunken, wailing song.

"Wanna go out?" Maria turns her soulful eyes to me, her long dark hair cascading around her shoulders. She and I have become inseparable this past week, ever since she moved in to escape a stalker at her apartment. My boyfriend introduced us, and we became fast friends. For days, we talked nonstop, not even pausing when one of us was in the restroom. We talked about our past, our hopes for the future, and the meaning of it all. "Let's go!" I answer, and we head down this street that has become home, for better or worse. And then, right between a lone drummer and a young crowd of laughing students, I see this giant green iguana whose humans are carrying her down State Street. She is magnificent. Maria lets me stop and hold her. Lizzy cuddles quickly into my sweater, and I cautiously place my hands on her back, my heart pounding so fast. I rub my finger on her head, and she closes her eyes. I am in love. I study the long spikes on her back, menacing-looking yet so soft. I trace her intricate scale patterns all down her back and long,

long, sharp tail. Maria is hungry, and Lizzy is cold. We reluctantly part, her human prying her nails from my sweater. I have been changed, and I am moved to tears. There are no words for what just happened. A species barrier has been crossed, and I suppose no words are necessary for that. I was finding love after terrorism, and that, my friend, *is* the big deal.

Not a week later, I brought Maria into a pet store. Looking back, I would not have supported the pet store industry, which has not been praised for its handling of reptiles. If I had to do it over again today, I would have helped a rescue center. But I have no regrets because I have my Samantha. On October 5, 2001, the pet store worker picked out several bright green wiggly babies for my friend and me to hold. We narrowed our search down to the tamest two. She liked the other one, but I liked my Sammy. Sammy was calm with both of us; the other one was less calm with me. And Sammy—oh fragile, tiny Sammy—never in my life have I seen such a sweet face! It was estimated that Sammy was between two and four weeks old. We will never know if she came directly from the wild or was bred in the states. Sammy's ancestors most likely came from Mexico, though it is actually possible that her origins are from Central America, the Caribbean Islands, or Brazil. All but Sammy's tail fit in the palm of my hand. Later, I measured her at less than fifteen inches snout to tail, and only four of those inches did not include her tail. She had a tiny, alien-like head. Her feet, it seemed, were already huge! She weighed only a few ounces. Once I held my Sammy to my chest, I had to take her home immediately. Her enclosure wouldn't fit in my friend's car. Even as the worker sighed and complained about the downtown traffic on game night, I insisted on taking her home, and I paid the worker to drive her enclosure out to my apartment after his shift.

As we waited for her room, I rested on my couch, petting her tiny head as she lay terrified on my chest. She was so scared; she did not open her eyes. I began to feel a tremendous responsibility for this fragile soul. And Sammy became quickly attached to me, reaching her shaking arms out for me when scared of visitors. As Wendy Townsend states, "The iguana's eyes are very expressive . . . according to wariness, fear, inquisitiveness, anger, hunger, and recognition . . . It is particularly moving to sit quietly and still with a baby iguana and establish eye contact with the little lizard. As he is beginning to get used to the human face, in his eyes, the expression of fear is almost completely replaced by what one might call wonder. When he grows up, his look becomes a look of familiarity and—I hope—contentment."[4]

I gave Sammy a day to adjust to her new home with me, but by the next day, when she still did not eat, I took her to a reptile veterinarian, who was pleasantly surprised to see such a tiny one. She explained that usually iguanas come to her as adults. Sammy did have a parasite from being housed with all of those other hatchlings in the pet store. I was given some white medicine in an eye dropper to feed Sammy once a day. I wondered how she would tolerate this first thing that I would ask her to do. She was perfect. Not only did she tolerate the medicine, she genuinely appeared to enjoy it. And Sammy looked so cute as she lapped it up. She became more alert and curious, making more tilted head movements and flicking her tongue. Her eyes became bigger, and, best of all, her everlasting smile was born. Sammy's wide lips turn up slightly at the ends, giving her the appearance of having a constant sweet smile.

During that first week with Sammy, a magnificent parade marched in the street in front of my apartment. The parade was in honor of those who had lost their lives in the terrorist attacks one month earlier. "The light shines in the darkness, and the darkness has not overcome it."[5] My little green girl was already a symbol of growth, hope, and optimism in trying times. Still, I never expected to fall so hard and fast in love with a lizard.

---

[4]   Frye, Fredric L. 1995. *Iguana Iguana: Guide for successful captive care.* Malabar, FL: Krieger Publishing Company.

[5]   John 1:5.

Six-year-old Sammy playing on her tree

. . . .

Let's Get Sambunctious

Yes, the green iguana is an unusual pet, and the topic of reptiles is often wrought with stigma. As a psychologist, let me digress for a moment. Contrary to some people's expectations, the mental health field no longer consists of ice baths, confinement, and other cruel and unusual punishment. I recall, on my internship, an older couple entering the behavioral health unit of the VA hospital with such trepidation that they would not even sit down in my office, much less close the door. They explained that their medical doctor's referral to our unit was a mistake, and they have never been, nor are they now, in need of behavioral health services. The comedy in the frantic nature of their exit was dampened only by their obvious discomfort.

The green iguana, known as *Iguana iguana*, on the other hand, may not have a history to warrant such discomfort. Unless, of course, we consider that they may indeed be descendants of the dinosaurs. At least one animal psychic is rumored to have discontinued doing readings with the iguana because, she dismayed, "All I get is world domination."

5

In any case, reptiles do tend to invoke, in a lot of folk, a great deal of uneasiness. Many people would not sit in a room with an iguana, at least not without experiencing some anxiety. The cold-blooded reptile is too often misunderstood as cold-hearted. When given a little extra warmth, Sammy is the most loving sweetheart. Just as mental health services can provide down-to-earth help, the green iguana exemplifies many important life lessons for those who are open to listening. Thus I embark on this mission, in part, to undo misperceptions about the green iguana. Even if I am misunderstood, the modern day psychiatric hospital is a step up from the insane asylums of old. I hope, of course, that I am not misunderstood, and that instead, I will be successful in sharing Sammy's light.

You might wonder, eleven years and thousands of dollars later, "Why did you get an iguana?" Iguanas are a good choice for people like me who have allergies to pet dander. Yes, iguanas not only "go green," they are also hypoallergenic. The clean and quiet iguana makes a good roommate and friend. Furthermore, some of my fondest memories are of my sister and me playing on the bedroom floor with our rather large collection of multi-colored stuffed dinosaurs. We had stegosaurus babies who "hatched" out of little eggs when we pulled the zippers. The big red one was the father, the big purple one was the mother, and so of course together they made blue babies. In spite of a relatively normal upbringing, we actually developed a rather involved family feud involving various chronic illnesses, arguments, and jail time, which together rivaled a Jerry Springer episode. This foreshadowed the days of projecting numerous psychiatric diagnoses onto poor Sammy. In sum, I have always had a true obsession with dinosaurs, and the stegosaurus happens to be my favorite. In high school choir class, my teacher even chose a quirky song for me about a "green dog"; it seems I was destined to have a green pet. From the moment I first knew of the iguana, I knew I must have one. The iguana looks like an adorable miniature stegosaurus. In fact, I am not the first person to refer to the iguana as the "dinosaur of the living room."

"Indeed, the very hairs of your head are all numbered . . ."[6] All of the intricate markings up and down Sammy were lovingly crafted by our creative Master. He smiled as he thought of her long, delicate toes and cute little frog legs. He showed such humor to give generous muscles on her plump frame. He gave Sammy an impressively thick and spiked tail. No two iguanas' markings are the same. I am so at peace as I study the thick black marking all around Sammy's lower back just above the base of her tail, up to the vertical ripples of dark olive green which look as if paint has dripped off of a thin brush. I can imagine all of these subtle shades of green paint mixing together on a palate, and a tiny brush playfully speckling the backs of her hind legs. I love to kiss the bumpy "armor" of her neck while inhaling her pleasant scent (like clean fresh air), and I am still surprised by how soft and delicate are the back of her thighs. I find it humorous how soft the spikes on her back are (like "fake armor"). Many people are also surprised to discover how nice Sammy's scales feel to the touch. The feel is indeed very different than the "slimy" assumption. Then there is the mysterious "third eye" on the top of Sammy's head, which looks like a miniature white light bulb. The third eye helps her sense heat and predators such as birds. Sammy's intricately patterned dewlap usually frames her neck like a soft necklace, which readily extends into a shield in courtship and other battles. The dewlap also assists with her heat absorption and prevents her from overheating. Sammy's triangular delicate jawline perfectly frames her soulful eyes. After all these years, I am still mesmerized by my beautiful dinosaur's prehistoric appearance. She looks quite majestic when her bright green scales glisten on a sunny day after we spray her with water for refreshment. Sammy is frequently referred to as a "darling," and I have taken to calling her my darling dinosaur, my sweet pea, my baby bean, and my sugar smacks. I like to tell Sammy, "You don't have to be so cute. Mama would still love you if you were half as cute!" And then, there is a quality about the way she holds her head with her body stretched out and upward, combined with that bright green color, knowing smile and bright eyes, that has made more than one person refer to her as "regal." It is clear that Sammy, although she is

---

6   Luke 12:7.

just one lizard, is the creation of a great deal of loving attentiveness. Be assured that we humans were also created from such a place of wonder, gentleness, deep purpose, and abiding love.

There is as much variability between iguana's individual personalities as there is between humans. I have completely fallen in love with my Sammy's personality. Sammy indeed seems remarkable, speaking as objectively as I can about it. Sammy consistently shines her light in the veterinary offices. Staff and customers openly express delight at seeing such a large bright green lizard who, in spite of displaying some nervous hyperactivity when at the doctor's office, maintains a smile on her face. Watching those smiles spread is like watching a sun rise. More than one reptile veterinarian has told me that she is the "sweetest" iguana the office had ever seen, and the "most well cared for." While those characteristics are undoubtedly intertwined, I also credit Sammy's sweet temperament. There is a reason, after all, that I chose her out of all those baby iguanas. I have more than a few examples of people who have previously disliked reptiles having called Sammy "adorable." And Sammy shows children a gentle attentiveness that accomplishes for them a validation of their unique importance in this world. This is one reason why I like to think of Samantha as an ambassador, albeit a rambunctious one. Many animals—reptiles included—are emotionally complex creatures. Sammy the green iguana shows us a range of nuanced emotions with her subtle and various nonverbals. Her facial expressions and body language are truly remarkable. Simply put, Sammy is an ambassador who helps educate us on how to love better. We just need to remind ourselves daily to listen. Sammy, the Sambassador. The Sambassador who gets Sambunctious. I know, I'm sorry, but you will see what I mean! These green friends work their way deep into our hearts.

Samantha [*suh*-**man**-th*uh*]

-noun

1. a <u>female</u> given <u>name</u>: from an Aramaic word meaning "listener."
2. Princess, or Pampered Princess
3. Queen
4. Darling Dinosaur
5. Sweet Tea Pie
6. Key lime pie
7. Sugar Smacks
8. Baby Bean
9. Banana Baby
10. Peanut
11. Big Fat Baby
12. Big Fat Girl
13. Green Girl
14. Green Angel
15. Green Machine
16. Sambassador
17. Lazy Lizard Lady
18. Rambunctious Reptile
19. Samazing Girl
20. Silly Sammy
21. Precious Doll
22. Lovely Lizard
23. Magnificent Creature
24. Good Samaritan
25. And, my personal favorites: "Girlfriend" and "Sweet Pea."

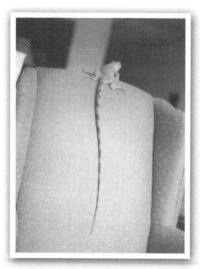

Sammy a few months after adoption

Common Questions

*M*ost captive iguanas do not live beyond their first birthday due to improper care. It breaks my heart to hear stories of iguanas who were tossed outside to freeze to death once they became "too big" for their owners. Our Sammy has reached her full height at 4.5 feet (now she is growing in the other direction, at a current 8.1 pounds). A full-grown adult male iguana can reach an impressive length of six feet. Before buying an iguana, please realize that having an exotic pet is an expensive and time-consuming endeavor beyond what most pet store workers will tell you. "'Men have forgotten this truth', said the fox. 'But you must not forget it. You become responsible, forever, for what you have tamed.'"[7] Speaking from personal experience, having an iguana is a serious commitment.

---

[7]   Saint-Exupery, Antoine, and Richard Howard. 1995. *The Little Prince.* Hertfordshire: Wordsworth Editions Limited.

When Sammy was a tiny baby, I would sometimes step outside of my apartment on State Street with her sitting high up on my shoulder, a leash gently wrapped around her body. She has always had a delightful effect on lifting peoples' spirits and bringing them together. Crowds of people would stop and fire away questions:

- "What does she eat?"
- "Do people eat them?"
- "How long do they live?"
- "Does she just run around your place?"
- "How do you know she's happy?"
- "Does she bite?"
- "How do you know it's a girl?"
- "Doesn't she want a friend?"
- "Do they like to be petted?"
- "How does she play?"

I enjoyed answering all these questions and showing off my new baby, until one day Sammy decided that she was brave and she wanted to explore the library mall. She leapt from my shoulder, immediately rolled out of her leash, and ran straight for the trees. Yes, they can run fast. I threw myself down repeatedly in the grass trying to grab her body. (Never grab an iguana by their tail; they can drop their tail but growing it back will be very taxing to their immune system. By the way, I have since learned that one way to stop an iguana escapee is by throwing a pillowcase over their head. Unable to see, they will stop long enough for you to retrieve them.) Sammy was still so tiny; I imagine onlookers who could not see her assumed I was having some kind of hallucination, seizure, or worse. When I finally got my Sammy I held her close, asking her what I would do without her and where she would go without me. Now we only take her outside if she is in a secure enclosure. We have tried various leashes and harnesses and she immediately alligator rolls out of every design.

I continue to enjoy answering all of these questions because the sooner we cover the basics, the sooner we can discuss the really important stuff. That is, Sammy is my green angel. Her ways have really taught me some important lessons at just the right time in my life. Throughout this book I have highlighted my answers to the above questions, which I think I can answer—if you will join me on a spiritual journey with one very special lizard.

Eleven-year-old Sammy in her outdoor enclosure

. . . .

Holistic Health

What does she eat?

Before we can achieve anything akin to spiritual enlightenment, we generally have to meet our basic needs of water, food, warmth, sleep, shelter, safety, and routine.[8] At least, it can be argued that a fully socialized iguana must first achieve these basic needs. A fully socialized iguana like Sammy, by the way, has become more than just a tame pet. A social iguana enjoys companionship as part of the family.

It is important that we eat healthy, and Sammy has done a remarkable job of encouraging us to make healthy food choices every day. The best source of expert information on the green iguana is Melissa Kaplan's

---

[8]   Maslow, Abraham H. 1943. A Theory of Human Motivation. *Psychological Review 50*, 370-396.

website and her book Iguanas for Dummies. [9] [10] Melissa is a brilliant and humorous writer. She has outlined the famous "MK Diet" for iguanas, which I will not duplicate here except to say that Sammy likes some ingredients more than others. What follows is Sammy's personalized diet, otherwise known as Sammy's IEP (iguana eating plan). Other great resources include Iguana Iguana by Fredric Frye, James W. Hatfield's Green Iguana Ultimate Owner's Manual, and the Green Iguana Society website, which includes nutritional information for every food you might consider feeding your iguana. [11] [12] [13]

Iguanas are true vegans, though they might opportunistically flick a bug on occasion in the wild. Sammy eats leafy greens and veggies and small amounts of fruit. Iguanas should never be fed any animal protein, as this is potentially very harmful to their health. Most all of their food should be consumed raw so as not to cook the vitamins out of the greens. Sammy's salad is made fresh every day and presented to her on her own special plastic dishes. We cannot leave the salad in her enclosure, as one might leave out food for their dog or cat, because Sammy's salads would quickly wilt under her heat lamps. Just as we humans are advised not to eat right before bedtime, Sammy needs at least an hour or two of basking after eating in order to digest her food. Since we buy large quantities of greens that tend to go bad before Sammy eats them all, we have started to cook some up for ourselves. Though they are too bitter for us to eat raw, Sammy has indeed inspired us to eat healthier.

As a petite woman at risk for osteoporosis, I credit Sammy with helping me eat more calcium and vitamin D. Since Sammy has become a part of my life, I have a constant supply of fresh fruits and vegetables. Sammy has always loved collard greens, which makes me very happy as

---

[9]   Kaplan, Melissa. 2013. "Herp Care Collection." Last modified January 13. http://www.anapsid.org.

[10]   Kaplan, Melissa. 2000. *Iguanas for Dummies.* New York: Hungry Minds Inc.

[11]   Hatfield, James W. III. 1996. *Green Iguana: The ultimate owner's manual.* Portland, Oregon: Dunthorpe Press.

[12]   Frye, Fredric L. 1995. *Iguana Iguana: Guide for successful captive care.* Malabar, FL: Krieger Publishing Company.

[13]   Green Iguana Society. 2013. Accessed July 24. http://www.greenigsociety.org/.

collards are a staple green for iguanas. She feels similar about dandelions (another staple green) but it is surprisingly hard to find dandelions that haven't been attacked with pesticides. Sammy used to like mustard greens more as a baby; I wish she still liked them as much because they are so good for her. She is fond of turnip greens, escarole, and the occasional endive, bok choy, and spinach. She loves her swiss chard, which is o.k. but not a staple green. She will select out of her salad, with her dainty tongue, the swiss chard pieces first. At times when she is offered a large swiss chard or collard leaf, she will even nibble on the large center stem like a dog with a bone (of course we do not allow this to continue, as she could choke if we did). Sammy tends to stuff herself with large bites of swiss chard. We often have to encourage her to swallow her swiss chard, as she tends to eat it so fast. We pause and demonstrate a swallow for her, and it works every time. After large gulping swallows, she sometimes stares at the chard longingly with a slightly open mouth as if wishing her stomach were larger (we think it is quite substantial enough already). Sammy also seems to particularly enjoy watercress, which her papa sometimes offers to her as a bouquet. It has been interesting to learn about the different properties of various leafy greens. For example, swiss chard is not a staple green because it contains oxalates, which can interfere with the body's ability to use calcium. Variety is important, as green iguanas can indeed distinguish between and appreciate the colors red, yellow, orange, and green. Sammy also refuses to eat greens that are not very fresh. In caring for Sammy's nutritional needs, I have become more aware of the need for variety in my own diet, as well as the meaning of the adage, "everything in moderation."

Yummy, yummy, yummy, in her baby iggy tummy! We tear leaves into bite-size pieces and then use a food processor to mix the veggies: green beans, sugar snap peas, parsnip, sweet potato, carrots, and squash. She likes her carrots more than her squash and I sure wish it was vice versa. Every now and then her salad is topped with lentils, or with fresh hibiscus flowers (hard to find but very good for her and she loves them). In the early evening Sammy eats her green beans or asparagus broken into little pieces that we hand her or set in front of her. Shortly before bedtime she occasionally gets a few moistened "figs for the ig", which she tears into with a dinosauric ravenous pleasure that sometimes requires a face wash. Iguanas should have fruit as a small portion of their diet, though some fruits are more nutritious than others. Figs are a good source of calcium. Sometimes, especially after coming back inside from the heat, Sammy will eat peaches, watermelon, or grapes. Bananas are only to be fed on rare occasions. Sammy has always been a banana baby; she will run across the room and sit in a stranger's lap if he is holding a banana. This is another reason we cannot let her outside unattended.

Three-year-old Sammy enjoying a rare banana treat

The last two days Sammy ate little. Each time we approached her with food she would lick it several times, and then she would turn her head away from the dish. Sometimes she even walked, with a swagger, through the salad, leaving a trail of leaves and processed veggies in the aftermath of what we like to refer to as her "spoiled baby attitude." We have learned that after giving Sammy the rare treat of a few small pieces of bread or pizza crust, she goes on a bit of a hunger strike, "copping a tude" with us when we then try to feed her normal food. I have heard of iguanas who become so "spoiled" on plain lettuce that they will refuse for weeks to eat the balanced diet they need. This is often more difficult for the human to tolerate than it is for the little green beast. This is also true of hand feeding. It seems iguanas, including Sammy, will become quite lazy on occasion, and practically insist on being hand fed all the time. Sammy's body language during these times reminds me of a toddler who did not get her way. She quickly turns her head away from the salad, then jerks her body away, and stomps through the leaves and into the bedroom. This attitude used to worry us, of course, until we learned. Now, we feed her far fewer treats, and when we do give her a treat, we roll with the subsequent "tantrum" with less concern. We also enjoy hours of entertainment giving Sammy a voice for these occasions, "What is this? Is this what I've been reduced to? I'm not eatin' that! You're kidding me! Where's the bread? Gimme the bread!"

I think that we have done a good job of not overindulging Sammy, though I cannot resist telling her that she is too cute for her own good. She is such a beautiful little princess with an air of entitlement and vanity about her.

Sammy would probably love to remind us of the importance of "daily bread," but perhaps bread should be fed to iguanas even more rarely than bananas. One difficult thing about having an iguana is that unlike animals that have been domesticated for years, we know less about caring for an iguana. How much is "occasional" or "rare"? We thought half a banana every two weeks would be o.k.; after all, she enjoys it so much. But we learned a lesson when one summer she started to hide in our bed a lot. It is o.k. for an iguana to, once in a while, take a nap after a big meal. Sometimes Sammy seems to enjoy taking a break from all stimulation as she crawls in between our pillows, leaving only her tail visible. But Sammy was choosing to hide instead of play, and we also realized that she had not shed in several months. Adult iguanas typically shed several times a year, while baby iguanas shed more often as their little bodies grow. A vet visit confirmed that her calcium to phosphorous ratio was off, so we cut back on the bananas to a half banana every two months, and we also concentrated on giving her as much outdoor direct sun exposure as possible. While the UVB (ultraviolet) bulbs above her indoor enclosure are replaced, as recommended, every six months, direct sunlight is still the best. Direct sunlight is simply the best at activating vitamin D in order to allow for proper calcium absorption (an important thing for both reptiles and humans to remember, indeed). Did you know that for us humans, just fifteen minutes of direct sunlight a day can also improve our skin, our immune system, our sleep, and our mood—just to name a few benefits? Sammy's ratios are back to normal (2:1 Calcium:

Phosphorous), her hiding stopped, and she began shedding again. And she really loves her time outside; she becomes the most enthusiastic about her salad when she is sun-soaked. As a result, Sammy has also taught me about health anxiety. At times, we are all inclined to avoid that check-up because we fear the worst. Sometimes, serious symptoms can reflect problems that are relatively easy to address.

How can we tell when Sammy is hungry? When Sammy is hungry, she appears restless and hyperactive, as if she is looking for something. She flicks out her tongue more often and she attempts to eat the carpet. At other times, she bobs her head at us. On still other occasions, Sammy might simply look at us. Perhaps each of these methods of communication represents a varying degree of hunger; we are still learning her language. If I had to venture a guess at the moment, I would say that when she bobs for food she is quite hungry. At those times, she tends to devour her food rapidly, causing vegetables to fly off her plate and onto her face and anything else that happens to be within several feet. Afterward, she kicks back her legs and stretches her belly, like a human unbuckling their pants after a Thanksgiving meal.

When Sammy does not want the food that is offered to her, she may close her eyes, walk away, or even tilt her chin up while shaking her head "no." She tends to do this with berries. Similar to humans, her tastes have changed over the years. She enjoyed watermelon as a baby. She refused it for many years, and recently began enjoying it again. Recently, I cut up some pieces of watermelon and set the dish in front of her. She took one look at it and walked right over to Zak's slice of watermelon, which the ig-wipped iguana papa obligingly held for her so she could eat her melon just like the grownups do. By the way, "Ig-wipped" is "the state of being beaten into psychological submission by your devotion to their every whim."[14] We certainly identify with many of these "wippisms," including the fact that my mom consistently refers to Sammy as her "green granddaughter," we grope around the kitchen in the dark rather than risk waking Sammy up after her bedtime, and Zak makes grocery store trips several times a week (sometimes more than once a day) to find Sammy the most fresh greens that exist in town.

---

[14] Kaplan, Melissa. 2013. "Herp Care Collection." Last modified January 13. http://www.anapsid.org.

Eight-year-old Sammy with her Christmas gifts from Grandma

Ten-year-old Sammy with her Christmas stocking,
made by her beloved friend and pet sitter

Well, what goes in must come out. Sammy takes a bath every morning for several reasons. Sammy very much enjoys daily soaks for about a half hour each morning. This is how iguanas naturally relieve themselves, and it is also the cleanest and most convenient for the iguana's humans. Once Sammy does her business, we simply scoop, flush down the toilet, disinfect the tub, and wipe that baby's bottom. Yes, in the wild, iguanas are extremely clean animals who actually wipe their own bottoms with the jungle's version of toilet paper: rocks. Iguanas are very good swimmers, so Sammy gets some exercise in her morning baths. In fact, iguanas are one of the few animals who can both climb and swim well. Iguanas can even stay under water for up to thirty minutes. Another important reason for a daily soak is that iguanas need a lot of water. In captivity, the health of their kidneys is at risk due to dehydration. Water also helps the natural shedding process. The iguana's natural environment, the rainforest, provides them with the constant water that they need. Of course, keeping a humidifier and always providing a clean water dish in the enclosure is also vital. We keep Sammy's salads well moistened, and we encourage her to drink from her water dish every day. Since drinking standing water does not come naturally to iguanas, Sammy requires encouragement to drink from her dish. Once she gets the hang of it, she often drinks deeply and then sits with her neck raised as she swallows. At other times, we might let water pool into a large collard leaf; as she chews the leaf, we gradually pour small amounts of water into her mouth. For a description of Sammy's daily routine, including detailed feeding and bath time instructions for Sammy's sitters, readers can visit Appendix B at the end of this book.

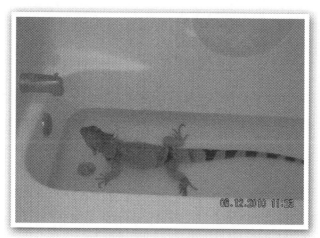

Eight-year-old Spa Sammy enjoying her bath

Do people eat them?

Yes, in Central America, iguanas are known as "chicken of the trees."

When I first brought her home, Sammy certainly seemed afraid that I might eat her. She would not open her eyes for several hours. I sometimes wonder if the night a few weeks after bringing her home marked the turning point in her fear. That night, she awoke startled from a sound sleep by me gently shaking her and asking, with tears in my eyes, if she was o.k. I had not realized how shallow the iguana's breathing is when they are in a deep sleep. I suppose she figured if I was going to eat her that would have been the time. Never fear, my sweet green dear. Now, I affectionately call to her, "Sammy, Sammy you're so sweet; Mama's little baby's good enough to eat!"

How long do they live?

Or, as some less-enthralled acquaintances have asked, "When is that thing gonna die?" If you are asking that question, my response is: "NEVER, SHE'LL NEVER DIE" (followed by maniacal laughter).

For the rest of you, I say that twenty to thirty years is a good estimate for captive iguanas. It is not known how long they can live in the wild, though it is understood that many do not live beyond their first year. They are fragile and the predators (mostly snakes and birds) are many. The longest lived pet green iguana to date, to my awareness, made it to the age of twenty nine (Don Burnham's Iggy).[15] Iggy was a big spoiled captive iguana. I like to fantasize about Sammy breaking that record.

Does she just run around your place?

Some iguanas, known as "free-roamers," do indeed run around the place. They must have a basking spot in order to obtain enough heat and UVB rays, and the home must be thoroughly iguana-proofed to prevent injury (they could choke on the back of an earring, or catch their fragile

---

[15] Hatfield, James W. III. 1996. *Green Iguana: The ultimate owner's manual.* Portland, Oregon: Dunthorpe Press.

toes in that pile of CDs as they leap onto the entertainment center). We choose to keep Sammy in her large 8' by 6' enclosure while we are away from the home.[16] This enclosure takes up half of our living room, and it is large enough for us to walk right in. Sammy seems to enjoy this mansion, as she even eagerly seeks it out at times. We have taken care to give her adequate room to stretch out in a soft hammock that was created by sewing a sweatshirt to a pair of jeans (we sometimes wonder if the seamstress is still scratching her head on that one). Yes, iguanas love soft surfaces. We often find Sammy resting on our bed or floor cushions, and appearing quite content to curl up beside blankets and her very own stuffed animal, her turtle buddy. Sammy also has a staircase and rock ledges which she can climb up and down if she desires drinking water. Once, my father-in-law helped us secure to her enclosure sturdy ropes, which she enjoyed climbing until the rope frayed. Sammy's lamps are separated by a hood to prevent her from burning herself or knocking them over, which can cause serious injury or even a fire. Some devoted iguana owners find investing in a UVB meter to be helpful, in order to measure the amount of UVB exposure their babies have at various spots within the enclosure. Iguanas need a basking spot of around 90-95 degrees Fahrenheit, and an ambient (air) temperature of approximately 80-85 degrees Fahrenheit (again, I defer to the experts, Melissa Kaplan, James W. Hatfield, and Fredric Frye, for detailed information on iguana lighting).[8] [17] [18]

---

[16]   Cages by Design. 2013. Accessed July 24. http://www.cagesbydesign.com/.

[17]   Kaplan, Melissa. 2000. *Iguanas for Dummies.* New York: Hungry Minds Inc.

[18]   Frye, Fredric L. 1995. *Iguana Iguana: Guide for successful captive care.* Malabar, FL: Krieger Publishing Company.

Sammy's indoor enclosure

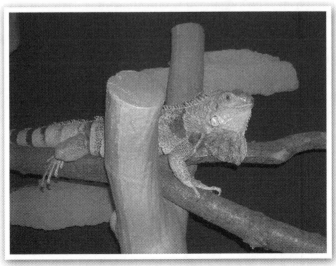

Three-year-old Sammy stretching out in her enclosure

Iguanas also enjoy a lot of sleep. Sometimes, Sammy takes an afternoon nap in between the pillows on our bed, or she snuggles right up with us. Sammy has been known to stand up on her hammock and push at the top of her enclosure with her palms; this is her way of letting us know that she would like her lights to be shut off early so that she can sleep. At nighttime, Sammy's UVB lights are set on a timer to automatically shut off while her heat remains on at around 80 degrees. She gets about ten hours of shut-eye on weeknights and twelve hours of sweet iggy dreams on each weekend night. What a life, right?

Sammy's enclosure must be regularly cleaned and disinfected. I love the laminate floor; it is easy to clean as well as some of the safest substrate for an iguana. When Sammy's Plexiglas walls look as if they have been sneezed on, it is definitely time for a thorough cleaning. Iguanas technically do not sneeze, though this is exactly what it sounds like when they snalt. Snalting refers to the process by which they eliminate salt from their little bodies. (Iguanas cannot sweat like us humans do.) Sammy's walls are simply wiped down with paper towels and water, while her hammock is washed and the rest of her enclosure is scrubbed with hot soapy water before it is treated with a safe animal disinfectant. When Sammy's hammock is being cleaned, she paces like a child whose favorite stuffed animal is in the dryer.

While we allow Sammy to run around freely indoors as much as possible when we are home, Sammy also has an outdoor 6' enclosure for the summer months. This enclosure is made of bamboo and mesh.[19] It is like a giant jungle gym for her, consisting of a mesh ceiling and walls and swinging bamboo ledges that she loves to climb and tear down. We are constantly securing this enclosure to ensure that it remains escape-proof, and we never let her out of our sight when she is Sunny Sammy. We love summer weekends and refer to them as Sammy Saturdays and Sammy Sundays. Sammy eats more on these days and so we also have Sunny Sammy Second Salad Saturdays and Sundays. There are few things more satisfying than watching my bright green dinosaur baby have fun in the sun while eating to her heart's content.

---

[19]   Lizard Cages. 2013. Last modified April. http://www.lizardcages.com.

Iguanas are escape artists. We know that if Sammy ever found her way out of the enclosure, she would likely run straight for the trees. We have no idea if firefighters rescue iguanas like they do cats, but we would really rather not find out. Sammy would not know how to fend for herself, and it is very doubtful that she could find her way home. We also watch Sammy closely so that we are immediately alerted if she begins to pant. Iguanas look like panting dogs when they are overheating. Even though the cold-blooded green iguana's natural climate is a hot and humid rainforest, these summer days in Missouri can still be dangerous for her. We try to prevent her from overheating, by keeping a towel over one corner of her jungle gym for shade and also by providing her with regular mists of cool water. As she receives the gift of water, she tilts her head back, extends her dewlap, and closes her smiling eyes. She turns very bright green and animated when she gets toasted in the sun, at times even appearing to threaten escape. Apparently, it is quite common for sun-soaked iguanas to become energetic and wild.

Even when home alone in her indoor enclosure, Sammy always has a lot of interesting things to view. Iguanas are visually oriented, similar to humans. While their sense of smell is probably keener than ours, they still rely mostly on their vision (including color vision) to obtain cues about their environment. Two turtles swim in a tank on a nearby table, and the woods behind our home are always teeming with the activity of birds, deer, and other interesting creatures. This enriched environment is especially important to the green iguana, who is actually quite intelligent for a reptile. Indeed, research has shown that for animals in general, mental stimulation is necessary for proper brain development. Sometimes, this can be as simple as shredding her parsnip in strips rather than processing her vegetables, just to "mix things up" a bit. She also likes it when the hearts of her escarole are ground up with her veggies. It is enjoyable for us, as Sammy's humans, to be creative in thinking of new ways to entertain her. We have experimented with television shows, and have discovered that while Sammy is a fan of Elmo, she tends to turn away with a look of disgust when Barney is on.

Sammy also appears to genuinely enjoy music, in particular, female artists like Abba, Madonna, and Portishead. She leans her bright green body forward toward the speakers, smiles, tilts her head, and blinks her big bright eyes. She has even been known to dance with her mama, who has chosen the Rolling Stones' "Beast of Burden" as Sammy's theme song.[20] She will never be my beast of burden, such a pretty girl.

And my darling dinosaur loves to have her head rubbed. Her head has remained rather small (we are still not convinced that it is large enough to hold a brain), to the degree that I can, with one hand, simultaneously massage the top of her head, her chin, and her dewlap. She visibly relaxes the muscles in her neck, closes her eyes, and sighs deeply when I do this. As she leans forward, it is necessary to have either a pillow or my other hand under her chin during these massage sessions. Her spa days also include a mani-pedi using a Dremel tool to file her nails down; no reservation required. Sammy is always very calm during the mani-pedi. She will often close her eyes and even hold out her hand or foot. We have found the Dremel tool to be the best way to trim her nails, as the risk of cutting too deep is reduced. It is very important in the days after trimming an iguana's nails to take care to "spot" them as they climb, lest they lose their grip and slip.

I often remind my clients that the mind and body should have never been separated. That they were ever conceptualized as separate is unfortunate, as it not only contributes to stigma with regard to seeking "mental health" versus "physical health" services, but it is also just an entirely false notion. How we take care of our bodies (with diet, exercise, sleep and relaxation) directly impacts our mood, and our moods also influence how well we take care of ourselves. Stress contributes to health problems, and health problems exacerbate stress. Sammy eats well when she has had a good day of playing and fun in the sun. And when she eats well, she is apt to have more energy for exercise. All of this goes most smoothly when she has all of her needs met, including the need to be mentally engaged with a view of the wildlife in our yard, music, a massage, and a kiss of sunshine.

---

[20]   The Rolling Stones, *Beast of Burden* (Paris: Pathe Marconi Studios, 1977), http://www.rollingstones.com/

Green girls: Seven-year-old Sammy with the author

Why Sammy Is My Green Angel

*T*he green iguana regularly survives forty foot drops onto the solid ground of the rainforest. How do we find strength in the unimaginable once that becomes a reality? As a psychologist, I have the unique pleasure of observing the full catastrophe in life: all of its pain, triumph, devastation, and resilience. It is a beauty to behold. As it turns out, struggles (both every day setbacks and the larger ones that knock the wind out of us) are actually opportunities to break through to growth. More important than growth is the burgeoning trust that growth will continue, and that the pain—whatever it is that we are going through—will, in its time, also come to pass. God gives us the tools when we need them. So, while it is difficult to imagine sometimes how we might overcome something, this is when trust is most important. At other times, I am tempted to minimize my own painful experiences, because they do not seem nearly as bad as many other stories of resilience I have witnessed. What we have not lived, we cannot imagine. What we cannot imagine perhaps always seems the worst, because we simply are not given tools that we do not yet need. The thing that is admittedly difficult for me to share is why I call Samantha my green angel:

I considered almost everyone at the barbecue a close friend; that is, until he arrived. He and I had met once, over a year ago at a friend's home. That night at my friend's home, he had requested several times that my boyfriend and I make out in his presence, and he then made several attempts to lure me alone. My firm tone and clear words went unheeded; it was actually necessary for me to push him away before he could reach me.

The night of the barbecue I was in a jovial, sunny mood. The night was peaceful and laughter came easy. Details start to get fuzzy here, but I clearly recall how warm I felt toward my friends and how safe I felt when I suddenly became aware of an intense feeling of nauseous intoxication.

I was disproportionately affected by the one beer I had consumed. I must rely on my friend's account, as I had amnesia for most of that horrible evening of sickness, incoherence and emotion. Some of my friends had to help me to the car, as I was not capable of walking on my own. I was like dead weight. Thank God for those true friends, who stayed with me and kept me safe from harm that evening.

I woke the next morning with painful stomach cramps. I was sick several times, and I was unable to stand for more than thirty seconds before collapsing with nausea and exhaustion.

Still, I did not consider the possibility that I had been drugged until I spoke with another friend of mine who had also been at the barbecue. He had asked this friend several times where my boyfriend was, and my friend had noticed something "creepy" and "anxious" in his tone. He also told my friend a lie about me: "She always thinks I'm hitting on her. Three times now she's said that." In retrospect, I realized that I had left my drink unattended once when I went inside to use the restroom.

When it occurred to me that he had intended his lie to be an alibi should I later accuse him of rape, a feeling of sheer panic and dread overwhelmed me. I thought of how close I had come to having my worst fear realized. I wanted to cry but tears would not come. The moment seemed suspended in time like a horrible nightmare from which I could not awake.

That night, I went to the emergency room where I filed a police report and talked to a doctor about my experience. "What makes you think you were drugged?" the doctor asked, disbelief in his tone.

I explained my symptoms, but the doctor insisted that date rape drugs typically do not cause nausea or vomiting (I later learned otherwise). He tapped my legs and arms, shrugged apathetically, and said he supposed it was possible that someone had slipped something into my food or drink.

In the days that followed I was overwhelmed by everyday tasks. At one point I was convinced I heard someone enter my apartment while I was in the shower. I sat huddled in the tiny bathroom with the door locked for almost an hour before I cautiously stalked the apartment with my cell phone. I slept a total of ten hours in four nights.

It took ten days for a detective to be assigned to my case. Finally, after five months passed without any investigation, I made the difficult decision to let it go.

By far, the most painful aspect of the whole ordeal was interpersonal. Some of my "friends" actually thought it was silly (and some other choice words) that I reported the incident at all, even though they knew that he had admitted to recreationally using GHB (a common date-rape drug). I felt very let down by the doctor, the police, and some of those who I had trusted to stand by me as my friends.

GHB is a clear, tasteless, odorless liquid known to cause amnesia, drowsiness, hypotonia, nausea, vomiting and lack of coordination. The onset of symptoms typically begins within fifteen to thirty minutes after oral ingestion. By itself it has been fatal, and it is especially dangerous when mixed with alcohol. These are facts of which the doctor at the ER was not aware or did not wish to acknowledge.

The barbeque and the aftermath of it occurred around the time of my transition between college and graduate school. At that time, I faced some unique challenges with my jobs, my boyfriend had just broken up with me over e-mail, and my neighbor was creepy: suffice it to say that I was depressed. It is very difficult for me to admit or even believe this now, but then, at my lowest, I truly wanted to end my life. I suppose the lifelong battle with thoughts of worthlessness and perfectionism (more on that later) was finally catching up to me. I had long held the belief that I was merely taking up space, and the fact that someone would go so far as to drug me in an attempt to use me for their pleasure seemed to confirm this belief. I made out cards and letters for family and friends, which were stacked in neat piles on my kitchen table. I will never forget my reaction to what should have been the proudest moment in my life, when I received the call that I was accepted into graduate school. I responded appropriately but briefly. I felt numb, because I truly believed that I would be long gone come fall. The problem was Sammy, who was less than a year old. Even if I found a method that wouldn't disturb her, who would care for the baby? My friend guessed my intentions when I asked him to care for Sammy if necessary. With all the warmth of a true "brother," he said, "No Emily, God has big plans for you," and embraced me as I sobbed. "'For I know the plans I have for you,' declares the Lord, 'plans to prosper you and not to harm you, plans to give you hope and a future.'"[21]

In the coming years, I published my master's thesis on drug-facilitated sexual assault, and I presented the findings at a national conference. I have also spoken to groups of young women at sorority events. All of this with the hope that I can help prevent this from happening to someone else. I say, "Please never leave your drinks unattended. If you do, dump it out. Do not let anyone buy you drinks unless you are watching that drink from the time it is poured until the time it is empty. Take drinks with you into the bathroom stall if you must. Always go out with a trusted friend. If you or someone you know is ill or becomes suddenly intoxicated, go to the ER and file a police report immediately."

Although I did not know it then, God was there all along. He was there in Sammy and He was there in my friend. Perhaps He sent them as guides during this time of struggle. Not long before this incident, a dog saved me from a different kind of insidious darkness. I was unloading groceries from the trunk of my car when a man suddenly appeared, asking a question about the parking meters that he could have easily answered for himself. He stood too close. As a feeling of unease rushed over me, my friend's large schnauzer (I was dog sitting) leapt to his feet from the back of my car, pushed himself into the trunk, and barked at the top of his sweet lungs. The man simultaneously leapt backward,

---

[21] Jeremiah 29:11.

muttering, "I didn't see the dog," and disappeared. I have always been quite certain that if it had not been for the dog, I would have been pushed into my trunk. I continue to struggle with the question of suffering: why would I have been spared, and where were the guides for the other lost souls? I certainly do not consider myself worthy to have received this help, and I do not believe that these blessings were born out of any action of my own. They were precious gifts, pure and simple, and they made me more aware of God's presence and love. "The Lord is close to the brokenhearted and saves those who are crushed in spirit."[22]

I have a spiritual connection to Sammy because she has taught me so much, including the most important message to date—this life is not ours to take. We have a responsibility to be here even when times seem extremely complex and we feel hopeless. In retrospect, I am embarrassed at my selfishness. Now, I try to consider that even the minor daily inconveniences may be blessings in disguise. When we experience ugliness and fear, we are reminded once again that we have a job to do. This was one of Sammy's first lessons to me. Sammy needed me, and through her big sweet innocent eyes and the way she tilted her head I was able to see this, even through the fog of the deepest depression. I do credit her and my other true friends with saving my life as well as infusing it with new meaning. Now, I am so grateful that nothing worse happened to me the night of the barbecue. I have learned to dwell on the positives, and there are many positive things that have come out of this experience. "Finally, brothers, whatever is true, whatever is noble, whatever is right, whatever is pure, whatever is lovely, whatever is admirable—if anything is excellent or praiseworthy—think about such things."[23] I believe that while God does not "let" bad things happen anymore than He causes them to happen, love cannot help but seep into all of those dark places. And when it does, it changes them forever. Maybe that particular darkness has become just a shade lighter. In any case, I know that in the daily struggle to discern God's voice, we can be assured that God's voice, while often still and small, does not guide us to live a life of fear or despair.

---

[22] Psalms 34:18.

[23] Philippians 4:8.

Five-year-old contemplative Sammy

• •

Emotional Intelligence

*O*ne of the most ill-fated artificial distinctions that has been made, alongside the separation of mind and body, is the idea that one cannot be both emotional and logical. It is more accurate to state that the most logical decisions we make are actually informed by our feelings. By observing Sammy's emotions, I have developed a greater appreciation for God's presence in all of the ups and downs of life.

Reptiles are often underestimated with regard to their ability to communicate and connect. Sammy has a wide range of nuanced emotional expressions. Sammy communicates with head bobs, color changes, and subtle movements of her body, head, tongue, and eyes. Her playful mood, for example, seems readily apparent to us now: bright green color, stretched out and active body, uplifted head, bright eyes, and turned up lips. I have learned from her to observe closely because the way someone communicates may not be as we expect. The iguana has a whole language of head bobs with which to communicate thoughts and feelings. Most probably, our intellectual functioning as assessed by Sammy's Head Bob IQ test would be no higher than the Borderline range. Sammy sometimes bobs very low and rapidly, and at other times with slow, dramatically large movements. Head bobs can mean a variety of things including but certainly not limited to, "Hello," "Play with me," "I'm hungry," "Time for my bath," "Back off," "I'm hot," or "Look at that!" She sometimes gestures with her tongue as if to show us something. At other times when we are bird watching on the deck together, she will bob her head, and when I look in that direction I see a magnificent blue jay or a deer. One time as we were sitting together on the couch looking out the window, she put her hand on my shoulder, turned her head toward me, and bobbed emphatically at a deer. The rush of air on my neck as her dewlap brushed against my chin is a feeling I will never forget, and the awe we shared as we observed yet another species is an experience that cannot be captured in words. I like to think that Sammy is pointing these beautiful things out to me. And whether or not that is her intention, it is most certainly the effect.

I continue to learn from Sammy every day. Recently, she opened her mouth in a brief pant, signifying that the lazy lizard was thirsty but wanted me to take her down to her water dish. After she drank, she began to chew on the carpet. She then ate the green bean pieces I placed before her, until deciding to go straight to the source, preferring to be hand-fed. She walked toward me with her lips slightly parted, her long tongue gently reaching for the beans. When she sauntered into the kitchen and placed her little front paws firmly on the floor as she looked at me expectantly, I knew it was time for her salad. She enjoyed several bites of her greens and vegetables. With carrot on her lip, she then came back for more beans. Next, she was off to the bedroom where she looked up and even reared up a little, like a horse. I made a little ramp with her turtle buddy to ease her up onto the bed, where we engaged in a rambunctious round of climbing play until she clung onto me. Feeling the slight chill on her belly and dewlap, I carried my sweet Sammy to her enclosure, where she reached up her arms and eagerly climbed into her hammock with one gracious pull-up. She basked for a while. After observing her tongue-flick her hammock and stare me down, I fed her some apple pieces. I have also witnessed Sammy communicate the full range of emotions:

How do you know she's happy?

I come home and see her bright green in her outdoor enclosure, one leg casually dangling off the swing. My lovely lizard strikes me as a beautiful teenage girl relaxing by a pool. She seems so content and her colors are truly her "happy colors." She rubs the side of her face on her swing, closes her eyes, and smiles.

Sammy brings joy and other fruits of the spirit. "The fruit of the spirit is love, joy, peace, patience, kindness, goodness, faithfulness, gentleness, and self-control."[24] While I am admittedly "green" in this regard, I have often likened Sammy's presence to that of a happy-go-lucky toddler. I broke my favorite necklace, and it only occurred to me later that I should be disappointed about that. All I could think of at the time was how I needed to pick up all those little beads off the floor so that my baby would not choke. Sammy, at eleven years old, still scampers from the living room to the bedroom with a sound that is decidedly like happy little children's feet. What joy, my love, what joy!

Sammy often turns a brighter shade of green while I pet her, giving the impression that I am rubbing the color into her with my one hand on her head and chin and my other hand on her back. Sammy appears especially happy when her stuffed animal turtle buddy makes a surprise appearance while she plays in a less familiar room of the house. She also turns a brighter shade of green and smiles more when I focus my attention entirely on her, not distracted by the less important things in this world. Once when I was engrossed in a book, I startled to find myself suddenly engulfed in lizard; Sammy had leapt onto me, beckoning me to play in her mischief.

---

[24]   Galatians 5:22-23.

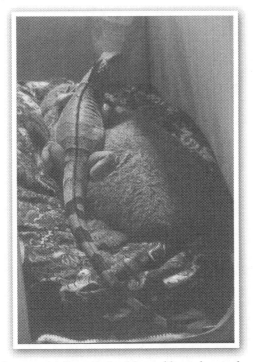

Five-year-old Sammy with turtle buddy and bean bag in her first outdoor enclosure. This enclosure now serves as her travel tent for vet visits.

Yes, at times, Sammy appears mischievous. For example, when she makes repeated unsuccessful attempts to climb certain things like my shelves of sweaters, she is seeking our attention. The way she pauses in mid-climb to look at us, head tilted, bright green and grinning, seems to add credibility to this interpretation. Sometimes I call her Samantha "Trouble" Jo, and request that she make good choices. If she gets so animated that she becomes difficult to redirect and I fear that she may accidentally injure herself, I playfully give her a "time out" in her room. She almost always becomes immediately calm in her familiar hammock under her warm lamps. Indeed, sometimes she practically jumps into her hammock, eager for a break from the overstimulation.

As Sammy has grown older, she has become even more contentedly docile. Sammy closes her eyes and sighs serenely. She even yawns sometimes when she is tired. As I carry her to her morning bath, her arms and legs dangle over the sides of my arm. I admire the reflection of her big fat belly in the mirror; she weighs about eight pounds just like a newborn baby. (To obtain her weight, I weigh myself both plus and minus the lizard, and subtract the difference.)

Seven-year-old Sammy

Fear:

Today I set Sammy on her heating pad on top of her window ledge in the bedroom. She enjoyed looking out the window until our neighbors came out on the deck. She tensed her muscles and lowered her head slowly so as to not be seen (she tends to "freeze" when she is scared). I tried to calm her by petting her head; she closed her eyes and relaxed her body for a little while. She never has liked dogs and humans within view outside our home. Since the little neighbor boy wanted to stay out and play, I moved Sammy to sit on our bed (when she has more distance she seems to feel a little more in control; typically she just avoids moving closer to the object of fear). Eventually she jumped up onto her cat tree. She hunkered down again a few minutes later; apparently the neighbor had gone inside briefly and then he came back out. Even when I closed the blinds, Sammy stayed hunkered for a good minute or so (apparently she does not abide by "out of sight, out of mind"). A little while later she lifted her head and looked toward the window with curiosity.

In many situations we have observed that if Sammy is afraid of something, it is usually something she sees. She may startle at a sudden loud noise, but that fear does not last like it does when she sees something that she instinctually believes does not belong in her world. Once while window watching from our living room, Sammy saw some neighbor kids playing with super soakers. I suppose to her it was the equivalent of witnessing a drive-by shooting. She jumped and ran so fast into the bedroom, she was under the bed before I could move. She was easily coaxed out with some banana. She sat still on the bed, blinking her big eyes in an apparent shock state. She recovered within twenty minutes and was back to playing and eating.

We have learned to keep Sammy away from the windows whenever the maintenance men have come by with the weed whacker. This machine really frightens her. Once, she even ran so fast that she did not look where she was going, and she bruised her little nose on the end of our bathtub.

Since birds prey on iguanas by swooping down on them from above, iguanas prefer to be high up in the trees. When Sammy was younger, she would run away from new people. Once, I lifted her high above my friends for several moments, and told her what a big girl she is. Afterward, she licked me and appeared to smile. For the rest of the evening, she climbed onto each of my friends instead of running from them. Having observed her surroundings from a higher vantage point, she was reassured of her safety.

I have learned to avoid wearing certain shirts around Sammy, as the patterns appear to frighten her. It seems that bright colors with a lot of horizontal lines or circles may be mistaken for the scales or eyeballs of a snake or another predator. We advise our Sammy sitters, should they notice Sammy puffing up her body and extending her dewlap, to assume that Sammy is reacting to their clothing patterns. I recall wearing a brightly colored floral tank top one brutally hot summer day; this day was particularly hectic as I was also the caretaker for Zak, who had just had an operation on his throat. As I mixed his smoothie and prepared Sammy's salad, I became increasingly aware that Sammy was unusually agitated. She looked wary of me and also as if she may fight me. I never allow myself to forget that she is, after all, a wild animal. In my hurry,

I threw on the nearest sweatshirt, which happened to be quite thick. I continued to prepare food and take frequent trips outside to spray the green beast lest she overheat. Within moments, I was overheating myself!

I sure wish that Sammy did not have to experience fear, especially the chronic "captive stress" that iguanas experience. At times, Sammy appears restless even when her most basic needs are met. She becomes immediately calm when we pet her, as if she has truly been craving that comfort. As she closes her eyes and leans into my hand, I think of how her biological parents abandoned her, and then she may have faced unspeakable horrors when she was captured to go to the pet store. At the pet store, she was housed with too many other baby iguanas in one small enclosure. She was terrified when I retrieved her, having not yet known that I would be her iguana mama. I pet her, watching her smile spread and her colors brighten as her head sways gently from side to side. Even though it is over eleven years later and she is now fully trusting of me, I remind her anyway that we have nothing but love for her. In the process of using soft speech and slow movements, which Sammy finds comforting, we have found the gift in living as calm and quiet people. It is, of course, most unfortunate that iguanas were ever taken from their homes in the rainforests. We cannot really recreate that environment. We do the best we can. We are grateful that Sammy is safe from predators, and she is in a loving home. We try to encourage responsible pet ownership for those iguanas that have already been imported, and we agree with advocates who wish to ban future importations. This ban would be in the best interest of the beloved green iguana.

Anger:

Does she bite?

Not anymore. I followed the expert advice on taming when Sammy, as a baby, did bite. Although her baby teeth did not hurt, and she even looked so cute doing it, I was reminded that adult teeth are somewhat less cute. In fact, an adult iguana can take your fingers off right quick. So, I took the information on taming seriously. Every time she bit, I raised my voice, "No! Bad Lizard!" and *lightly* tapped the top of her head. The purpose of the tap is to provide the quick motion coming down from above, the motion that is instinctually fear-provoking to iguanas due to the fact that most of their predators are birds. And iguanas do respond to tone and other properties of voice (for some evidence, check out a scientific study involving how iguanas respond differently depending on who is reading them a children's book).[25] In my personal experience, Sammy reacts in a certain way when I "baby talk" to her: "How did you get to be so cute? Did you have a cute mama? Did you have a cute papa? I bet you had a cute mama and a cute papa, didn't you?" She tilts her head and looks at me wide-eyed, innocent, and sweet.

I was consistent in taming; thus, within weeks I never again had to tell Sammy that she was a "Bad Lizard." Did you know that "dinosaur" literally means "terrible lizard"? Of course, much of the taming process also involved the daily interactions: giving her massages and baths, hand feeding her, and carrying her around with me. Iguanas are "greener" when they are younger. I am not just referring to their color (though the babies are indeed a brighter green than adults, who tend to grey like us humans do). Sammy also became wiser around three months of age, as reflected by her more efficient and gentle communication. If she did not want to be picked up, she would turn away. If she was open to being held, she began to rest her hand on mine. "When I was a child, I talked like a child, I thought like a child, I reasoned like a child . . . And now these three remain: faith, hope and love. But the greatest of these is love."[26]

As a juvenile, Sammy's voracious appetite sometimes caused her to express irritability. If I did not have her breakfast placed on her table at 9 a.m. sharp, she would look at me, nod at her table, and then look back at me again. Other times, she would sit on her empty food dish and stare at me with an angry "green glare" in her eyes. Then, she would literally jump into her salad and devour it. That hungry little girl was growing. By her first birthday, she had doubled her size, measuring

---

[25] McRobert, Scott P. 1999. "Cues affecting human recognition in a captive iguana." Paper presented at the 36th Annual Meeting of the Animal Behaviour Society, Lewisburg, PA.

[26] 1st Corinthians 13:11-13.

thirty one inches snout to tail and eight inches snout to vent (the vent is the baby's bottom, and the purpose of this measurement is to illustrate the length of her body sans tail). As the years go by, Sammy has become increasingly muscular. My strong baby pulls herself out of the bathtub and holds onto me now, whereas I used to be the one holding her.

Sometimes when Sammy is shedding, she gets a bit fussy about being handled; for example, she might irritably push our hands away with hers in a quick, jerky backhand motion that results in her slapping her own belly. The body provides us with many opportunities for lessons. For Sammy, her periodic shedding reminds us to continually let go of past hurts and open ourselves for new experiences. Iguanas shed their scales in patches. Sammy currently sheds every few months; she shed more often when she was a baby growing out of her skin. Usually at least tolerant of being held, if not practically melting in our arms, when she is a Shed Head she often wiggles right out of our grasp. At other times, she may "give us lip"! Yes, the scales of her lips shed, at times in my hand as she leans into me and gently rubs her shedding face and even eyelid on my hand. A good clue that she is open to this is when we observe her tilting her head and closing her eyes while rubbing her little face on her hammock.

Sammy has also expressed anger when in pain. We learned to keep our laptops far away from Sammy after she trapped one of her long nails into the USB port. Sammy had run over to the computer in a playful mood, attempting to sit in my lap. Her nail became stuck in the side of the computer, and as she twisted her body the entire nail was pulled off. She sighed quick deep breaths with her mouth slightly open; this expression of pain and anger is sometimes referred to as a "green glare" or "open-mouthed stare." We dabbed her wound with cornstarch to stop the bleeding, and we treated it with Neosporin. Her nail grew back. Remarkably, she has also injured the end of her tail to the degree that it had to be clipped by the vet, but this also grew back. For many years, the tip of her tail had a bend to it, which eventually straightened. Now, the only evidence of injury is that the tip is missing stripes.

Sammy has prevented us from experiencing pain. One time, I was inside with Sammy while Zak was outside on our deck. Sammy had been watching Zak from her perch on the back of the couch. All of a sudden, she leapt onto the patio screen door. I had never seen her do such a thing. Confused, I gently pulled her off. Zak quickly came inside, explaining that Sammy had scared off the hornets that had surrounded him. Good girl!

On another occasion, some of our friends helped us move a couch. Our tallest male friend had a fear of reptiles, and he decided to cope with it by immediately demonstrating his "dominance" over Sammy. As Sammy innocently sat in her hammock safe inside her enclosure, he suddenly moved toward her and towered over her as close as possible. She puffed up her body nice and tall, dewlap extended, and *hissed* at him. We have never heard her hiss before or since. Our friend backed off. I was so proud of Sammy.

Sammy provides excellent examples of how to use anger appropriately. Anger informs us that there is a boundary that needs to be established: between her and the laptop, between her and others, between the hornets and Zak. Sammy expresses her anger just enough to point out the need for space, but she does not overreact to the situation, nor does she indulge her anger. In my work, I have learned that many of us have a difficult time differentiating between assertiveness and aggression. On the one hand, we sometimes say mean things in the name of assertiveness, without considering a calmer approach. At other times, we hold back from expressing our needs because we fear that we may be perceived as demanding. While it can certainly be argued that we humans face more complicated situations than Sammy does most days, I believe that the image of her approach provides a powerful reminder to be appropriately assertive.

Sadness:

Our first vacation away from Sammy was difficult for all of us. Sad Sammy anticipated our absence much like any other pet. In fact, she jumped on top of our luggage and looked up at us with the most forlorn iggy eyes we had ever seen. We have been very fortunate to have excellent Sammy sitters who care for her so that we can visit our families. On one of our vacations, Sammy's sitter observed her to run up the stairs and repeatedly knock her head against the closed bedroom door in an apparent attempt to find us. Her sitters gave her extra love, bananas, swiss chard, and massages. Sammy appeared sweetly excited upon our return, giving us lizard licks after looking at us back and forth with quick little head movements and big eyes. I have included our "Sammy instructions" for pet sitters at the back of this book.

Disgust:

Sammy responds to most berries with disgust. She shakes her head quickly from side to side, giving the appearance of shuddering. She closes her eyes and turns her head away. She has sometimes pushed the dish away.

Envy:

She's green!

Surprise:

Sammy seems to like to eat and play around 5 p.m. every day, around the time her papa arrives home from work. Sammy does "double takes" when she sees someone she is not expecting. For example, on the rare occasions in which I reach home before Zak does, Sammy literally does a double take. I am the first to wake up, and I give Sammy her baths. On the rare occasions in which Zak is the first to see her in the morning, she looks at him, looks away, and then looks back at her papa again, with a slight startle reflex in her upper body.

Sammy is used to being bathed first thing in the morning. One time when Zak was up early, I sat next to him on the couch and we talked about our plans for the day. We were not talking for long when Sammy looked directly at us and emphatically bobbed her head. Joking that she was agreeing with an offhand remark I had made referring to myself as a freak, I carried the baby to her bath where she immediately did her business. She was probably also agreeing with me.

If Sammy is surprised to be picked up, the feisty girl might swing her tail and "spank" us. By the way, if you ever find yourself in this position, here is a tip: hold the iguana in close to your body. That way, there is less kinetic energy behind that lizard tail whip, and therefore it smarts less.

At times when Sammy's brain seems to be working hard to figure out something in her environment, she looks all around with wide eyes, and she moves her head more quickly than usual. Her head remains tilted, and she often looks up toward the ceiling. Often, her mouth is slightly open from just one corner. On other occasions when she is inquisitive, she explores the room by flicking her tongue. Her tongue allows her to both smell and taste her world.

There are many variations to Surprised Sammy. One day, Sammy sat on the back of the couch with her eyes bigger than usual and her mouth slightly opened and rounded. Her head was very still. Then, closing her mouth slowly and slightly moving her head straight back, she looked at me with still-big eyes, the smile returning to her face. I looked into the face of my green angel and cherished her all-knowing, everlasting smile. I realized that she was surprised because I had turned on music; yes, it had been too long since I had played music. A simple yet powerful message was communicated from heaven above through a green iguana named Sammy.

11-year-old Sammy with the author

Seasons

ammy and I first moved together from Wisconsin to Ohio when she was less than a year old. We moved so that I could begin graduate school in Ohio. Sammy rides in a mesh tent carrier designed for large dogs. On the long drive, I had to pay close attention to the temperature. I sprayed Sammy with water whenever the bright sun threatened to cause her to overheat. She seemed confused, and she did not eat on the day of the move. For several weeks, she explored our new apartment by flicking her tongue and tilting her head, her wide eyes and slightly open mouth revealing her confusion. She stopped doing her business in her bathtub and made messes in her cage. I attributed the loss of her toilet training to the stress of the move. I kept trying new things and reading more books and chatting with other iguana owners, but still daily I was coming home to fecal smears. At that time, I was a single woman in my first semester of graduate school in a new town, and I was stressed. At the height of my frustration, it actually occurred to me that I might not be able to handle a pet. The thought immediately flooded me with guilt. I continued to struggle with frustration and guilt until one day after much prayer I decided that no matter what, Sammy and I were in this together. I would stick by her through all the poop. Her problems continued, but now I felt different. I no longer was consumed by negative emotion because I knew we would find a way through this. Only then did I start to hear her. She needed more space. She had outgrown her 75 gallon terrarium as well as her baby bath tub. She received an 8' by 6' mansion and began taking baths in the human tub. With rare exceptions, she never had an accident again. This experience has provided a useful (though perhaps not very popular) metaphor for other relationships. Once we express a willingness to be in the tough times together (and yes, even to put up with a little poop), we might be able to suspend our own feelings long enough to hear what the other is saying. In retrospect, I am very appreciative of Sammy's assertiveness. Because she communicated her needs, I have more respect for her and we have a closer relationship.

"Love is patient, love is kind . . ."[27] As I review this book, I notice how many times Sammy has waited for me to do things that are undoubtedly very important to her. Sammy, my lazy languid lizard, serves as a good model of patience. She does not become angry if I am a few minutes late with her bath or dinner. She waits with her amused smile for me to play with her. She peacefully observes the wildlife from her window sill ledge in our bedroom, often kicking back a limb or two, her sizable belly spreading underneath her. Her peace is tangible. She tilts her head to the side and slowly moves her eyes with a remarkable combination of innocence and inquisitive wisdom. Her manner of curious observation is truly a gift to behold. Sammy's gentle watching and listening is a wonderful reminder to approach relationships with curiosity rather than frustration or judgment. Sammy reminds me to become curious about other perspectives even when I do not understand or agree. "I am still confident of this: I will see the goodness of the Lord in the land of the living. Wait for the Lord; be strong and take heart and wait for the Lord."[28]

---

27   1st Corinthians 13:4.

28   Psalms 27:13-14.

In retrospect, Sammy prepared the way for me to love. I was in my first year in the clinical psychology program when Zak caught my eye. He was an advanced graduate student in the social psychology program, and he was quite the cute professor when he came to our class to teach us how to create a webpage. He was patient, generous, and positive. Of course I needed a little extra assistance with my webpage; in particular, I needed help turning Sammy's photo collage into a slideshow. Zak happened to love animals, I noticed right away. I also noticed his intelligence. The very next day, my friend Carol stopped me in the hallway. Carol was known for her astute intuition. She asked, "Do you have a boyfriend? Or girlfriend, I don't want to make any assumptions?"

"No, I don't!" I laughed.

She continued, "I've been thinking, about Zak. Do you know him? I have been thinking about you and him."

I was astounded. "I've been thinking the same thing!" I exclaimed. I could hardly contain my excitement. Carol offered to have us meet at her place for dinner. She informed me the following day that Zak preferred to take the initiative. He did, and the day after our first date he drove me in a severe snowstorm to retrieve my friends from the airport. They were enamored with this adorable sweetheart who was rescuing them; they had been prepared to stay the night at the airport. No other cars were on the road, and we stopped frequently to remove the thick snow from the windshield wipers. The hour-long drive took several. At the end, in my apartment driveway surrounded by a pure white winter wonderland, we shared our first kiss.

Zak instantly assured me of his gentleness and remarkable attentiveness toward our Samantha. And Sammy clearly loved Zak from the start. He passed the iguana papa test with flying colors. Sammy, playfully leaping on him, riding around on his back, and nuzzling his chin, became the happiest I had ever seen her. Her color became bright green, and her eyes shone above her wide smile. Truly, her quality of life improved with Zak's help in assembling and cleaning her new enclosure, fixing her fancy salads, designing a hammock, investing in and maintaining the best lights and the best humidifiers, and implementing more structured human interaction time—you get the picture! Samantha is our little green princess. And the way she often leaps into our arms in a loving embrace, she really seems to be a grateful little child. To this day, she looks for Zak if he is not home at his usual time, and she seems happiest when all three of us play together.

One-year-old Sammy with Zak the iguana papa

How do you know it's a girl?

On this beautiful fall day, I carry Sammy around as she looks out the windows. Sammy seems to want a treat instead of her salad; she keeps wandering around, following us into the kitchen, and flicking her tongue. Of course, she may be looking for a place to nest because she does not understand that she no longer has eggs and in fact has no ovaries. At least these behaviors are much less intense than before her spay. Before her spay, we force-fed her at the recommendation of the vet, who advised us to keep her hydrated when she refused to eat. We would wrap her in towels, and one of us would gently pull her dewlap to open her mouth. The other would squirt the mixture of nutritious food and water into her mouth. She would often shake her head from side to side, sending the green "baby food" all over us and the bathroom. We didn't care about the mess, but we did care that she did not seem to like the whole experience. We just wanted the best for her.

Iguanas reach maturity anywhere between their second and fifth year. We did not know that Sammy was a girl for about three years after she came into my life. I had always called her my little girl; Sammy's look and markings are decidedly feminine. She has a dainty, delicate way of selecting her leaves with her tongue. She has been called sweet and petite. I would have been surprised if she had been a boy. As she matured, the vet remarked that her smooth jaw line and petite build was most likely that of a female. One day, she refused to eat, and she frantically searched for a way outside. For weeks she seemed full of energy; I would place her at the bottom of the stairs and then meet her at the top and "run" her back down. I was trying to get her energy out so that she would stop bruising her little nose and injuring her tail on her enclosure when her need for heat (or our need to be out of the home) necessitated her being enclosed. Sammy had eggs in her, and she was desperately trying to find the right conditions to nest. Iguanas, like chickens, make infertile eggs (from twelve to thirty at any one time). Sammy's eggs were causing her to become anorexic and extremely stressed.

At our vet's recommendation, four-year-old Sammy was spayed. This vet was very skilled in caring for reptiles, and for years when we lived in Ohio we drove an hour each way to take Sammy to him. After many hours of surgery and an overnight stay, Sammy returned to our home with a light stomach, a scar from her chest to the bottom of her belly, a bright green color, and a proud iguana mama. I gained respect for her strength when I saw all the dozens of eggs lying on the table. She had been carrying around all those eggs for months, and yet she never was mean. The day after surgery was one of the most playful days she has ever had. Her iguana papa was quite worried, shaking his head, "Running around the day after surgery!" For weeks, I "sealed" Sammy's tummy with Vaseline before her baths to prevent infection until the stitches came off during her next shed. Sammy is tough and she carries herself with integrity and dignity—that's how I know she's my girl. Well, that and she is often caught jumping into my purses, jewelry, and shoes.

Doesn't she want a friend?

I feel sorry for Sammy that she had to go through all that without so much as even looking at a male. In captivity, mating iguanas is, well, a real mess. The eggs, the dozens of eggs, require a complicated incubation system. Ethically, given how many unwanted iguanas already exist, I would not want to bring more into an unnatural habitat. And as far as housing iguanas together, there are serious risks of them becoming territorial and not abiding by a "sharing is caring" philosophy with regard to heat and food. They can become quite violent toward one another, even fighting to the death. In the wild, while baby iguanas do tend to huddle together for safety, adults generally prefer to be solitary. In any case, the iguana experts are unanimous that an iguana should reside alone within its captive habitat, and many experts strongly prefer that only one iguana reside in the household. We have never even entertained the possibility of another iguana, as we know that we simply do not have the space, much less the resources, to fully commit to and love a second iguana in the way it would deserve. Similarly, it is too risky, in our opinion, to have another pet like a cat or a dog which may not get along with our Sammy. Of course, there are many examples of people who have done a wonderful job raising multiple iguanas and other pets. Sammy remains content to be our "only child."

The three of us (me wearing a diamond ring containing green emeralds in honor of Sammy's central role in our relationship) moved from Ohio to Missouri after I completed my graduate coursework. In Missouri, I began my internship and postdoctoral residency at a VA hospital. Sammy's large enclosure requires a lot of big strong hands, some planning, and for me to just avoid looking. While we are now able to move the enclosure in sections, the original construction of the mansion literally caused blood, sweat, and tears for us and our fellow graduate students.

Five-year-old Sammy with Zak and turtle buddy on moving day in Missouri

Sammy's quality of life improved in Missouri's sunnier and more humid environment. Sammy usually has a few days when she can step outside as late as November and as early as March. There have even been surprise days in January when the temperatures have soared into the upper 70s. Living in Missouri forces us all to enjoy the moment because it is not unusual for the temperature to change by thirty degrees within a day or two. On some days, I seriously consider bringing a change of clothing to accommodate the drastic temperature change that is sometimes anticipated in the course of a work day. Sammy used to appear downright depressed in the northern winters. I am also "solar-powered"; just like Sammy, I notice that my mood is certainly more cheery when the sun is out. In Missouri, Sammy still has a bright green color and serene smile in the winter months. She is still playful, more so on the sunny winter days compared to the dreary ones. She no longer reduces her food intake in the winter. We have also noticed that Sammy appears to pack on some extra, uh, layers on her belly shortly before winter begins. The green iguana could threaten the groundhog's career; just observe how much the green beast eats in early February to decide how much longer winter is lasting. I also believe that Sammy has become more adaptable with age and experience. Sammy has come to appreciate that seasons must occur.

Eight-year-old Sammy reaching for the stars

· ·

Resilience

I smile at the irony that a creature without vocal chords has helped me find my voice throughout the seasons of my life. The first two years in Missouri, I struggled to remain positive as I worked at the VA hospital, which I experienced as a male-dominated hierarchy with low morale and minimal validation. It is hard to pinpoint any one thing that was difficult for me, but it is interesting how, in retrospect, I see that I was in survival mode. I felt extremely fatigued most of the time. I felt an odd mixture of being overwhelmed and bored at the same time. A brain fog set in. I was taking prescribed sleeping pills that I now think were a part of the problem. Although I took it as prescribed, I am a small person who probably needs a smaller dose, or, as it turns out, none at all. At the time, I was filled with such anxious energy that even with the pills I would sometimes experience intense insomnia. On some nights, I even tried to release the energy by jogging in place in the middle of the night. Other factors were the constant construction, which caused headaches and possible exposure to asbestos. I also did not have an office, and even in my postdoctoral year shared the "intern den" with several others. The den was a closet with a heavy door in which were crammed six cubicles with no desk space beyond the keyboards. There was very little air flow and we could not hear the emergency alarms. If we said anything, we were not so subtly accused of complaining. I understand that the space issues have since been resolved. In any case, it was not the right environment for me.

At some point, I began to experience what I now imagine Carol Gilligan, Ph.D. was referring to in her writings about "loss of voice." This phenomenon has been observed in young women who come to realize that the world operates in terms of power dynamics, and women do not possess the power.[29] I certainly felt disempowered in the VA environment. I am not a big fan of war, and it scares me when large angry men who own weapons behave in a threatening manner toward me. I am not a tough-looking person by any stretch of the imagination, a fact that I was reminded of daily. I am also, for the most part, a mild-mannered and soft-spoken person. But something really happened to my voice when I worked at the VA. It became hard to choke out words in almost every context, even when on the phone with my family. People would often ask me to repeat myself, and they would lean forward straining to hear me. They looked almost shocked at my soft voice. I was self-conscious about the content of my words, the phrasing of my words, and the tone of my voice. In conversations, there would be lengthy pauses as I grasped for just the right words and tone. My health suffered; my stomach was a wreck, my mouth was dry, my heart raced, and indeed I felt on the verge of panic at times. The fear was compounded by the realization that others really could sense my fear. Throughout all this time, even when I was blocked from communication with every person, I could be myself with Sammy. She was a constant nonjudgmental presence, always bringing that tilted head of curiosity to her wide-eyed innocent smile. Sammy continues to help me let go of self-consciousness, as I never tire of observing her compelling appearance and behavior. I have learned that it is not possible to be self-conscious when we are truly observing the gifts in front of us. Love overcomes fear.

---

[29]   Gilligan, Carol. 1982. *In a different voice: Psychological theory and women's development*. Cambridge, MA: Harvard University Press.

Looking back, I think that spending time in Sammy's tranquil presence primed me to listen to the voice of one woman working the cafeteria at the VA. This woman was an angel to me. One day as she made my burrito, she exclaimed that she saw the light of Jesus around me. I felt a powerful surge of joy to realize that my Jesus was right there all around me, and I called out to the woman that she just made me feel the best I have ever felt in my life. She answered, "It's not me, it's God." She added that I was helping *her* right now by responding in an open way, because, as you can imagine, not everyone does. She asked me if I was in the church choir, and she told me to join. Before I could speak another word, she wrapped my burrito and walked around the counter. All the other employees and customers seemed to fade into the background. She then proceeded to address all my innermost insecurities—the worries that consumed me, which I held close to my heart. "When you look at people and sometimes they have a look on their face that you can't read, it's not about you. Don't worry about what they think. Be yourself. Speak your mind." Her embrace left me filled with intense love and joy that overflowed as I floated, beaming, back to my work. On my way, I learned that I had been touched by the Holy Spirit, and this love cannot be contained within the body. I saw a former intern in the hall and embraced her. I immediately shared my experience with a close friend, and we grinned from ear to ear. The feeling was truly the best I had felt in my whole life. I had never seen this cafeteria worker before, and I never saw her since.

I continue to learn from this experience, and I am probably not done learning from it. I have come to realize that in the presence of Sammy during my darkest days, I prayed for God to give me confidence and to heal my anxiety. Even when I did not have the words to pray, ". . . the spirit himself intercedes for us with groans that words cannot express."[30] God not only answered my prayer, He gift wrapped it with the exquisite packaging of gentleness, kindness, and compassion. And not only did He give me the gift of my answered prayer, He abundantly included even better gifts than what I asked. In fact, they are quite extravagant gifts. He gave me increased awareness of what the Holy Spirit feels like.

---

[30] Romans 8:26.

He showed me His generous spirit. He encouraged me to help others believe in the power of prayer, and He gave me the story to share. The story affects everyone in an individual manner. For my mom, it affirms her belief in angels. One of my friends said that my story helped her recognize how she had missed opportunities for similar experiences because she was not open to them. I did join the church choir, and some of the members were struck by the courage that God provides us. God showed me another layer of my purpose in this life. And I am still reeling from the fact that He is present for me and for all of us, and that He comes to be with us and love us.

Of course, my problems did not go away overnight, but the process had certainly been jump started. Some of my colleagues and supervisors at the VA passed along very helpful advice. For example, to "act as if" I feel confident; essentially, to concentrate on the behavior and the feeling will follow. It did. More importantly, there were many very good people at the VA who made it clear that they believed in me. Gradually, after beginning my work at my current position in a community mental health center with a wonderfully warm and accepting group, I began to say what is on my mind. With every breath away from anxiety, my ability to focus on helping others has deepened. Now, I recognize survival mode when I see it in a client. I believe in exposure therapy for social anxiety. I can testify that getting a degree in clinical psychology and teaching a class is one way to do it. Sammy is a topic of conversation that naturally puts me at ease. Perhaps others sense this, which is why they seem to enjoy asking me about her. And, of course she is simply fascinating. Sammy frequently finds her way into the content of my lectures on graduate assessment. I tell my students to carefully observe, as much of communication is nonverbal, subtle, yet very powerful. I show them pictures of Sammy demonstrating every type of attitude, emotion, and activity level. I teach them to observe with curiosity and without judgment. On every semester evaluation, at least one student requests, "More Sammy pics!"

I also had to work hard at uncovering the root of my self-consciousness. For almost twenty years of my life, I had told myself several times a day, "I hate you; you are no good, stupid, ugly, and worthless; you should just die." I am hesitant even now to acknowledge that I was ever so cruel to anyone. It is amazing to me that my negative self-talk went on for so long without my awareness of its impact on my mood, my behaviors, and my health. Actually, it was such a habit that I had lost sight of the fact that I was doing it at all.

One of the most important things I have done for myself is to replace the harsh inner critic with a voice of loving acceptance. Of course, that would not have been possible without my growing awareness of the unconditional acceptance of God, my beloved friends, and my family including my green daughter. With the guidance of my graduate school mentor, I gradually and consistently replaced each message of self-hatred with loving affirmations. Sammy was with me throughout this whole process, guiding me into awareness of the fact that I love her for simply being her. My acceptance of Sammy is not based on how "good" she acts today, and there is nothing that she can do that would change my feelings for her. As children of God, we are loved even more than we love our own children.

It is not enough to stop saying mean things to ourselves; we also have to fill ourselves with love.[31] As I now tell my clients, the key is patience. It did not help to beat myself up for neglecting to catch a critical word. Much as my mentor predicted, it took about a year to replace the habit. It worked. And once I began to reap the benefits of having replaced this way of thinking, a snowball effect occurred. I began to appreciate the energy and drive that perfectionism brings. I gradually decreased the size of my daily lists. Perhaps most important, I started to make time to appreciate the accomplishments I have made with regard to the perfectionism. After all, the irony of trying to let go of perfectionism is the pull to try to be perfect at letting it go. Of course, this is all an ongoing journey. Currently, my task is to embrace the perfectionism with acceptance and even gratitude. I do credit a lot of my growth in this journey to my mentor, in addition to a brilliant little questionnaire and book called the Strengths Finder.[32] This book is a fantastic tool for raising self-esteem while giving practical suggestions on how to build on our own unique individual strengths.

---

[31]   Luke 11:24.

[32]   Rath, Tom. 2007. *Strengths Finder.* New York: Gallup Press.

Now I tell my clients, "You are the only person that is guaranteed to be with you for the rest of your life. So be a good friend to you." I do not think I had much credibility with some of my clients until I started taking risks to share more of myself. For example, I was working with a talented and intelligent young man. He was empathic and generous, yet he just flogged himself on a daily basis (some details of this case have been altered to protect client confidentiality). Listening to the hateful things he said to himself conjured up painful memories of me not that long ago. Perfectionism is a significant problem for many people. Convinced of never being good enough, perfectionists struggle to acknowledge their accomplishments. Examples of failures are used as evidence that we will *always* fail in *all* situations. The perception of failure is easy to achieve for perfectionists, who consistently set unrealistic standards. Perfectionism is so many heavy things, and together it feels like a constant pressure. Perfectionism, at its core, represents an abandonment of hope for unconditional acceptance. Once we stop believing that we can be embraced for who we are as fallible human beings, we have given up on hope for true love. Of course, no one makes a conscious choice to be a perfectionist. But the process of letting it go is terrifying. It is truly difficult to drop the erroneous idea that we can control others' affection for us. The real risk we are taking is that we will be exposed as unlovable.

The beautiful self-critic before me could only see his strengths as weaknesses; indeed, he thought that his strengths were fundamental flaws of his character. We worked for months on logically challenging these thoughts. He hesitated to make time for himself, though he did allow tiny scribbles of a "journal" in the crowded boxes of his busy day planner.

As I worked with this young man, I thought about Sammy. Sometimes when Sammy swings on her outdoor ledges, she hangs by one foot and carefully views her options. She has to take a leap of faith to avoid staying behind, but she must also remember from where she came. Similarly, I needed to take a risk. While not hanging on to my past too tightly, I also needed to reflect on my own journey. So I shared my story with the young man. Really, all that I shared was that I used to say mean things to myself, I learned to replace those self-critical messages, and it has made a very significant and positive change in my life. He became moved to tears. He expressed gratitude that I would share this piece of myself, adding that it was quite helpful to be reminded that I was also "human." He pondered that someone who he perceived as undeserving of self-hatred had shared his struggle. In retrospect, I think that session marked a turning point for him because he began to consider that he himself might also be undeserving of self-hatred. He then began to really challenge his thoughts, and he did so with excitement and creativity. I watched with stunned amazement as he transformed into a confident yet quirky young man with affirmations on post-it notes all over his apartment. I myself was moved to tears the day he brought me a gift: a post-it note that pronounces in large bold letters, "YOU MATTER." I knew then something of the gift from God that we sometimes call resilience. It should not surprise us that the form it takes is a full circle. Sammy's circle thus began by her saving my life, and then teaching me to let go of perfectionism, self-consciousness, and fear—lessons that I, alive and well, continue to share with the voice she helped me rediscover. I contemplate these lessons as I rest with my big baby cuddled into my sweater, much as Lizzy was that day when terror had come to our nation and small sweet Sammy came to be my symbol of hope.

Playtime with eight-year-old Sammy, pictured here with both her parents

• •

Mindfulness And Relaxation

*L*istening to God begins with observation. As we observe Sammy's unique features and ask questions with an open curiosity, we learn that there is much more to her than we may have expected. Mindfulness, defined as "paying attention in a particular way; on purpose, in the present moment, and nonjudgmentally," is a useful psychology concept that Sammy helps teach us.[33] Here are just a few examples of how Sammy teaches us to observe and enjoy the moment.

This June evening Sammy laid lazily in her swing outside as the sun continued to shine. She enjoyed the wildlife in our wooded backyard (all kinds of birds, bugs, butterflies, owls, bunnies, and deer). A small bird, his orange hair straight up and his orange-red lips full, hopped all around the rail of the deck in a semicircle around Sammy's enclosure. This cutie

---

[33]   Kabat-Zinn, John, and Thich Nhat Hanh. 1990. *Full Catastrophe Living: Using the wisdom of your body and mind to face stress, pain, and illness.* New York: Bantam Dell.

tilted his head to the side and kept his mouth open as he studied Sammy from every angle. All he needed was little glasses and he would have been unmistakable as an avian science professor. Sammy, the sun on her side, tilted her head back toward him. I caught an amused smile on her green lips. How delightful to watch God's beautiful creatures enjoy each other! I think, as Jesus decided to come, he looked around at all this beauty. He realized he wanted to share it with us, forever, no matter the cost.

One of my favorite mindfulness practices that I started is to open each day with an attitude of gratitude. "Gratitude is not only the greatest of virtues, but the parent of all the others."[34] Gratitude feels like a concept that is hard to grasp, perhaps because it is so vast. There are an infinite number of blessings, and the variety of ways in which we are blessed is astounding. But thinking about gratitude is interesting because it also requires us, to some degree, to imagine life without those blessings. To me, being grateful means that I shed a sense of entitlement and recognize grace as the ultimate gift. That is, I do not really "deserve" blessings, even though this idea is not a popular one in this world. It is a choice to appreciate the things that are so easy to take for granted. "Store up for yourselves treasures in heaven, where moth and rust do not destroy, and where thieves do not break in and steal. For where your treasure is, there your heart will be also."[35]

Sammy, who enjoys sitting outside in the early evenings, has also inspired me to begin watching the sunset. Doing so, I am practicing mindfulness by focusing on the different ways in which the sun and the clouds and the sky take form each minute (and the subtle variations of the sunset each night). All around and within the woods is a cacophony of birds and insects, while distant dogs and children announce their presence. I breathe in the crisp air and pray: Lord that I may be open to love, receiving and giving, and open to forgiveness, accepting and living.

There is always so much to be thankful for, and when I train my focus on the positives, the rest falls into place. If the negative news coverage begins to overwhelm me, I look at good news websites like

---

[34]   Cicero, Marcus Tullius. 2008. *Collected Works of Marcus Tullius Cicero.* Charleston, South Carolina: BiblioLife.

[35]   Matthew 6:20-21.

the Daily Good. Even if I wake up feeling run down in the midst of a stressful time, I try to be thankful to have a roof over my head. I am thankful for the promise of a new day. "To me every hour of the light and dark is a miracle. Every cubic inch of space is a miracle."[36] I find that this focus inevitably leads to a desire to help others. I feel so grateful for another day, another moment, and another opportunity to give. After Sammy's bath I keep my gratitude journal and read my devotionals over cappuccino as she watches from her hammock with a peaceful yet intense attentiveness that I find especially endearing. I cherish those moments in the early quiet of the morning as we start our days together. Sammy reminds me to listen, observe, and relax.

Do they like to be petted?

Do lizards relax? Are they lazy, languid creatures?

Today, after she has had enough direct sun for at least part of Sammy Saturday, I bring her in and she runs to our bedroom (her favorite place to play). She stops in the living room and pauses, then bolts straight to the bedroom at a loud scamper. The noise reminds me of a rambunctious running naked toddler. She jumps onto our bed and sits content in a sunny spot while I cradle her chin with one hand and pet her head with my other hand. She sighs deeply, and her neck visibly relaxes into my hand. She tilts her head to reveal a wide smile. I inhale her deep earthy scent while I kiss her belly, elbows, knees, and neck. The only other time I have had the pleasure of this aroma is when walking on our nature trails on an early spring day. Sammy smells especially delicious after a day in the sun. It is almost an addictive scent, and I think of how close we get to others whose scent we adore. The intimate relationships with those we love the most often involve scents (our parents' baking, grandma's perfume, our lovers, our friends). Sammy's earthy scent strengthens my bond with her. I kiss her and tell her over and over how much I love her. I want badly for her to always know that. I am pretty certain that she is a lizard who feels loved, if not lucky.

---

[36] Whitman, Walt. 1973. *Miracles: Walt Whitman's Beautiful Celebration of Life.* Kansas City, MO: Hallmark Cards.

Sammy always looks especially cute in the morning, with a sort of innocent and expectant look in her eyes. I wonder if she has been dreaming and what her long sleep was like. Every morning I pull her out of her hammock and carry her to the bath. She enjoys swimming laps and often sits in the warm water with her arms kicked back and her eyes closed like she is having a spa day. Sammy especially likes water trickled over her head. Once after we returned from a weekend getaway, we found Sammy very content and relaxed. She felt like a rag doll. Our Sammy Sitter explained that she had given Sammy a full body massage that morning in the bathtub.

How does she play?

Every now and then there are moments too magical for words. On Monday evenings before I teach my class I alternate between playing with Sammy, feeding her, and feeding myself. One particularly memorable evening, she sat on her window ledge and rapidly bobbed her head. She turned completely around and emphatically bobbed with her face close to mine. I immediately put my laptop away. As I continued to make efforts to feed her various things and still the bobbing continued, it occurred to me: she just wanted to play with me; she wanted my attention. I picked her up and carried her all around the downstairs. I held her up high to look out the windows from all the different views. My precious baby melted into my hands so perfectly. By the time I left for class, I had beautiful fresh images of us nuzzling, her following me around the home, bobbing her head and then tilting it to look up at me—always with a smile on her face, a sparkle in her eye, and her entire body a bright miraculous green.

I like how Sammy plays more human-like than most animals in that she is in a different mood every day. On most days she is quite energetic with a proclivity for climbing. As a baby, she could rapidly climb straight up our brick living room wall. She would also regularly climb the carpeted back wall of her enclosure. She climbs us just for the sake of climbing, and she appears to "show off" as she jumps from the window ledge to the bed. She looks so proud when she does that. Mischievous Sammy looks first to see if she has our attention before she jumps in an off-limit location. I like how she runs into the bedroom to play and then comes out to look for one or both of us if we don't follow her. At other times, she abruptly leaves the bedroom and runs up the stairs to play in a different room for a change. Sometimes her papa encourages her to take an iggy back ride; he gets down on all fours, and Sammy jumps onto his back. She looks especially adorable as she rides around on her papa's shoulders; her muscular chest and biceps bulge as she threatens to leap and climb onto anything within reach. She especially likes to climb both of us at the same time, and she gets very bright green when she does this. At bath time, she swims gracefully and sometimes stands and walks against the edge of the bathtub as if doing a stair master in water. Sammy is lively and charismatic.

Seven-year-old Sammy catching up on her reading

When Sammy was about three years old, it appeared that we had misplaced her in the home. Where could she be? If it were not for her majestic long tail, I would not have found her where she had crawled inside a pair of my blue jeans. Miss Samantha Green Jeans, yes, you do wear the pants in this family. When she is not wearing my jeans, she is "wearing" her own, from her perch high above us in her hammock made of old blue jeans.

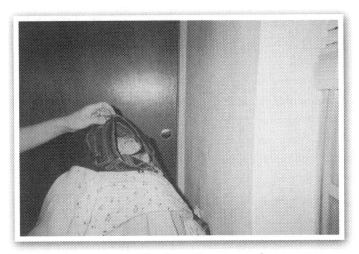

Miss Samantha Green Jeans, age three

Sammy delights all her caretakers with her playfulness. One time, Sammy's sitter fed her dinner while we attended a faculty meeting. The note upon our return read, "Sammy gone wild! Bobbin' her head in the mirror, scaling the cat post with big leaps, even jumping onto a rock in her cage." While some iguanas tend to get very stressed by mirrors, Sammy seems to like to look at herself in the mirror. We even set up a small staircase (designed for older dogs to climb into bed) in front of the bedroom's full length mirror just for her, because she was always seeking out the mirror. Sometimes she stares in a zoned-out state, while other times she treats her reflection like another iguana to be nodded at and nuzzled. We have more than one photo of her aptly depicting narcissistic vanity. After reading the Sammy sitter's note, I immediately rushed downstairs and opened her mansion. "Sammy did you hurt yourself with all your crazy antics?" She turned around on her hammock and climbed up her rock ledge. Observing her full use of all limbs, I thanked her for showing me that she was alright.

Sammy schedules play dates with our coworkers and new friends, who have the honor of meeting her and watching her show off. She truly seems to pose for pictures, and she generally becomes more animated for guests. I like to think that she has some time to prep when I say, "Sammy, your *friends* are coming over." At least, her eyelids always look like she has a turquoise shadow very expertly applied to accentuate her soulful eyes.

Sammy even plays with a stuffed animal, turtle buddy. We knew that Sammy would like her turtle buddy the first time we saw it in our friend's basement. Our friends gave it to us, and after we took it home and washed it we observed that our intuition was correct. Years later, Sammy still enjoys sitting on the soft green fluffy turtle-shaped pillow while we carry her around on a "magic ride." She also enjoys climbing her turtle buddy when he sits vertical against the wall. She wears her bright green happy colors when she sits on her fluffy friend. Sammy appears to understand that many times when she sits on her turtle buddy, I pick the two of them up and carry them around to look all around the home. Since I consistently pick her when she climbs her turtle buddy, I reason that she must like that or she would not keep playing this game.

Sammy engages in many forms of climbing play. Sammy likes to leap from her window sill onto "her" chair and climb up her cat tree. Usually she just hangs out from her high vantage point. On other occasions, she does something so wild it literally requires a time out in her enclosure. One time she leaped onto my dresser and slid across it at a remarkably fast speed. The next thing I knew, I had myself a leaping lizard skating in thin air. Miraculously, she landed on her feet without injury. Perhaps she had too much sugar (fruit) that evening.

Sometimes Sammy will also engage in more passive relaxation, such as crunching green bean pieces while watching an interactive children's book about iguanas on Zak's iPad. Yes, this really happened.

Sammy also loves to play outside in her mesh and bamboo enclosure. She swings on her bamboo ledges and climbs straight up and down the mesh walls. She gets excited and bobs her head. She becomes very animated, moving quickly all up and down and around in a very entertaining and monkey-like manner.

When I get sucked into painful news about all the missing and abused children and young women, Sammy turns her back to the television, runs back to the bedroom, and encourages me to get in touch with my inner iguana and just come enjoy the moment with her already. She encourages me by acting as if she is about to impale herself on the nightstand from a precarious grip on the bedpost that she has just slid down, much like a child on a banister. Yet she waits for me to "rescue" her by picking her up or letting her climb my arms or her turtle buddy. She waits for me with her hands on the nightstand and her head tilted, smiling at me. This has come to be known as "The Game", as Sammy does it over and over and appears bright green and even more smiley than usual while participating. She grasps at the wall behind our bed, pretending to fall but looking more like she is doing aerobics, until we come and save her from herself. I love to hold her while she sits on her turtle buddy all sprawled out with her bright green belly looking especially plump. She looks happy, tilting her head from side to side as I carry her and her buddy all around the downstairs level. She is comical and gentle all at once, and I feel the stress of the day evaporate. I cannot seem to get enough of her hugs and kisses. Sometimes when we are playing, my snuggly Sammy will stop mid-climb and put her arms around my neck, nuzzle my chin, and lick my cheek. Interacting with her is a panacea for any day's stress. On Mother's Day in 2013, Sammy suddenly paused during playtime, placed her hands on my chest, tilted her head, and looked deeply into my eyes. I felt like the luckiest iguana mama in the world.

One summer evening, I was changing out of my work clothes; I put on some shorts and closed the closet door. I heard what sounded like a hanger falling inside the closet. I opened the door and met the smiling gaze of my green girlfriend sitting in my laundry basket, her hand scratching the door. I had thought that she was back in her enclosure; Zak had just stepped out of the bedroom and he said that she was on the bed when he walked out. Silly Sammy! She seemed very pleased with herself. We both kissed her quite a bit; we were so amused. The next day, she was admiring herself in the mirror when Zak began reminding her of her time in the laundry basket. She immediately walked over to the basket! On other occasions, she has jumped inside the laundry basket and turned very bright green as I carried the basket of lizard up the stairs for a change of her playtime scenery. Sammy has been known to help me with the laundry on many occasions. Her help consists, of course, of walking through the pile of clothes as I fold them, and sitting on some items for such a long time that I have to nuzzle her to get at them. I simply cannot imagine a better helper.

We think that Sammy watches us with a curiosity about us humans' fast pace and focus on work over play. It is probably impossible for her to believe that anything could be important enough to rush around for every day. And when you think about it, it is hard to argue with her. Are we really supposed to be rushing through life checking things off lists, with an inbox that will never be empty? Sammy might say, "Why don't you just zone out in your hammock all day?" As she rests on my shoulder, her tail dangling between my arm and my side and her foot cradled in my hand, I bury my face in her sweet aroma and I think, "Reverence for God adds hours to each day."[37] Sometimes we do need to slow down and enjoy the process. If we believe in an eternity, then it seems we were made to enjoy the process. It can't all be about outcomes or finishing our lists. If it were, eternity would have an end.

"I know that there is nothing better for men than to be happy and do good while they live. That everyone may eat and drink, and find satisfaction in all his toil—this is the gift of God."[38] Sammy has taught me that there is more time to play than I had once thought possible. I think that I had almost believed that being relaxed was a guilty pleasure, as if feeling good was a warning that something was wrong or misguided. For years, this belief had masqueraded as its seemingly more benign cousin, perfectionism. Perfectionism is driven, of course, by fear. It has been difficult for me to make time to do the things I really enjoy like writing. I had thought that I needed to get everything "more important" done first. Now, I am starting to see that our inbox is never empty, and we are doing good just to keep everything we juggle in the air. Sammy has no place to be and she makes no qualms about it. Notice that guilt and shame were not on her emotion list. Animals seem to have a simple trust that God will take our smallest efforts and create something so beautiful that none of us could even handle a direct glimpse of it.

Perhaps my lazy languid lizard is really quite busy calling my bluff on distractions like time pressure, workaholism, perfectionism,

---

[37]   Proverbs 10:27.

[38]   Ecclesiastes 3:12.

self-consciousness, and—underneath it all—fear. Of course we are afraid to bare our souls in this world. When I write, it feels like I am exposing my bare naked soul with full awareness that some can and will trample on it. It will hurt. But what will hurt even more is if no one pays it any mind at all. Rejection stings. We could all be amazing artists if only we could let go of the self-consciousness that holds us back. The more I counsel, teach, and write, the more I feel drawn to dig deep and share what touches my heart. It is then that I often experience the feeling of the Holy Spirit, and I just know that I am right where I am supposed to be.

In any case, my life with Sammy is making me ask questions. The more questions I ask, the more I seek a relationship with God. I find that the Sabbath tradition helps us listen for God in many ways. In our playtime sessions with the green girl, we rest and celebrate life. We embrace a process of life that is not linear. Sammy really is an ambassador in the true sense of that word. She teaches us that if we cannot set aside a whole day every week, even an hour will give us many blessings. We might discover that when we make this time, we no longer feel stuck on that writing project, we know what to say to that client, or we have an idea for a friend. Most importantly, we stop having unrealistic expectations for ourselves and for others when we realize the unconditional love of God. As I write, I find myself being pulled into the light, and hope is renewed.

Always my green girl

· ·

Love

I mentioned that Sammy has a unique connection to children. When Sammy outgrew her first enclosure, she gave it away with royal green gentleness to a family of seven who eagerly returned her smiles. The couple had driven hours with five children (ranging in age from five to eleven) after seeing our newspaper offer of a free reptile enclosure. The children had just been given a baby iguana, and we took the opportunity to show them how big theirs would grow and the care she requires. Each child was allowed, with adult supervision only, to enter the enclosure without shoes. Each child was also required to wash their hands before and after petting Sammy. The children behaved flawlessly. I recall Sammy's particularly regal position that afternoon; to some of the children she might have seemed like a princess in a fairy tale. Sammy sat upright, her dewlap slightly extended under a very friendly smile. Her colors were a majestic emerald. Each child squealed with delight as Sammy closed her eyes with pleasure at their head rubs. The day was warm and sunny and shiny smiles were all around for hours.

It never ceases to amaze me how love is the essence of all important life lessons. Love is the closest answer I have to the meaning of life. God is love. When we love others, we are listening to God. When we listen, we observe love.

A Day in the Life of Sammy:

After my bath, I go outside and eat my salad. I get quite animated while soaking up the sun, and I climb around on my ledges and walls. My parents spray me with nice cool water before I get too hot. Whenever I am getting hot outside and I get a shower, I ravenously devour my salad. After I eat, my papa brings me in, kisses me, and gives me some banana—my favorite! I must be a good girl. I have to run and see for myself how cute I am. I stare at my mirror for a while and then I get a glimpse of my turtle buddy, so I jump on top of the bed and cuddle with him. I get curious about the wildlife outside so I jump over to the windowsill. Then I get comfortable again next to Mama on the bed. I kick my arm back while Mama kisses me and gives me a nice head and neck massage. It sure isn't easy being green, but somebody's got to do it. To emphasize how much I rule, I climb to the top of my tree. Then Mama has to come baby me and wash the banana off my face. I don't mind though. It feels kind of like a prolonged massage. I close my eyes and lean into her hand. She cradles me with one arm under my belly and the other wrapped over me. I rest my hands on her arm. After a while, I can feel myself being kissed and carried into my hammock for sleep and . . . sweet iggy dreams.

My wish for Sammy has always been that she feels love. Gary Chapman writes of five love languages: words of affirmation, acts of service, gifts, physical touch, and quality time.[39] Usually, the way we feel loved is similar to how we are most comfortable expressing love. For example, I have a strong preference for words of affirmation. I enjoy giving others' compliments, writing notes of encouragement, and finding new ways to lift a friend's spirits with words. I feel most loved when others do the same. The challenge in life is to learn how to both give and receive in love languages that come less naturally to us.

---

[39] Chapman, Gary D. 2010. *The Five Love Languages: The Secret to Love that Lasts.* Chicago, IL: Northfield Publishing.

In particular, it is important to learn our loved ones' languages. While I prefer words of affirmation, my husband identifies most with acts of service and physical touch. Although he is a man of few words, it helps to remind myself that every time he makes a meal or touches my hand this is love. Thankfully, with a nonverbal (actually a generally non-vocal) creature such as Sammy, I have many opportunities to practice serving with my actions and giving massages.

A Day in the Life of Iguana Mama:

Later that evening after I bring her inside, Sammy watches me play with the barrette in my hair. She jumps off the bed and climbs the staircase in front of me. We look at each other in the mirror. After a few minutes, I lay back on the bed and resume my writing. She travels down her staircase and looks up at me. Sammy suddenly leaps onto the bed and sits on my chest. I love these moments and I never want them to end. At these times, I feel quite fulfilled and blessed. Sometimes her big hazel eyes stare deep into mine. I really wish I knew what she was thinking. I have noticed that there is a pattern to these sudden embracing leaps. Sammy looked deep into Zak's eyes for a long time shortly after she received her new indoor mansion. She embraced us after receiving her outdoor enclosure. She also hugs me at more random times, and every time is equally delightful. At such times, I have no choice but to stop writing and embrace her, nor do I want to do anything but pet her, laugh, and smile.

Eight-year-old Sammy helping the author write this book

"Have we eyes to see love is gathering?"[40] Do we notice the gifts of love? Do we really notice that joy, for example, is a gift of love? Do we consider that every time we receive an affirmation, it is a gift of love? Yes, Sammy has expressed gratitude toward us with endearing lizard hugs. That first day she became my pet/guide marked the first of many cherished occasions when she seeks me out and rests on my chest, nuzzles her head into my neck, closes her eyes, grasps my shirt collar with her little hands, kicks back a leg, and breathes those soft little sighs under her serene smile.

Ah, to lie on the bed on a sunny warm September Sammy Saturday, the windows opened to the sweet smell in the light air while I pet a relaxed green head and upturned lip. Sammy slowly moves her head back and forth and relaxes into my hand. If this wild iguana can literally come to trust me with her very life, surely I can let go and trust God to handle my light and momentary troubles.[41] Although it is inevitable that Sammy's body will one day no longer be with us, her lessons will endure forever.

---

[40] Collective Soul, *The World I Know* (Miami: Criteria Studios, 1995), http://www.collectivesoul.com

[41] 2nd Corinthians 4:16-18.

Sammy's trusting lean reminds me, "Trust in the Lord with all your heart and lean not on your own understanding; in all your ways acknowledge him, and he will make your paths straight."[42] Indeed, there are many wise lessons that Sammy teaches us humans. In a card she received after one of her many play dates, her friend remarked that Sammy "put on a wonderful display of reptilian wonder." Sammy is often a peaceful and playful topic of conversation that brings people together. I cherish each moment and remember that the seasons are always changing. As she climbs onto my shoulder and pushes her smiling face close to mine, our eyes meet and I vow to always remember to appreciate the small things in life, to play, and to bask in joy.

I hope you have experienced how Samantha the listener teaches us love in its purest form. Now, think about the word "Love" for a moment. Have you noticed that the word itself seems to evoke a sense of the peace that transcends all understanding?[43] The word love crescendos into a roaring, crashing wave with that powerful 'v' sound, which reminds me of the conviction that is necessary in love. Indeed, it requires strength to continue to turn toward love in the difficult times. It takes a strong faith to not lose hope that the light always overcomes the darkness. The word love ends in a receding wave with a silent e; love is a return to eternal peace where there is no fear. Love is a circle of connectedness which transcends all barriers, even those between the green iguana and her humans.

---

[42]   Proverbs 3:5-6.

[43]   Philippians 4:7.

Sammy's Spirit

I had just finished writing when Sammy became sick. The timing was truly uncanny. I am grateful for that timing because I would not now be able to write about her life with the joy and humor that was her legacy. Sammy went from a robust and exuberant girl to a very sick iguana very suddenly, and she was gone within weeks. Iguanas are prey animals who instinctually remain stoic until their illness has become quite severe. Thus, by the time symptoms are noticed, it is often too late. The first sign we had that something was wrong was that Sammy began to swallow excessively and with difficulty. We took her to several reptile vets who could not find any signs of her having swallowed anything foreign, though all signs initially suggested that she had. Testing by multiple iguana experts including an out-of-town specialist yielded no clear answers. All we know for sure is that Sammy had liver disease caused by some kind of infection. There was a Cyclospora outbreak in fruits and vegetables in Missouri around the time she got sick, but we will never know for sure if this was the culprit. Though I think a part of me will continue to struggle for a long time wondering if I did something wrong or could have done something more to save my baby, postmortem testing has ruled out any obvious causes. It remains a mystery even to the experts. By the time she passed, we were relieved that she was out of pain and had passed peacefully. It was her time, so God took that angel girl up to heaven to spread her wings even wider.

Throughout the nightmare of Sammy's final weeks in illness, I recognized that I was being taught to trust, surrender, and let go. Of course, I first broke out in hives and lost my appetite and ability to sleep.

There continue to be a lot of tears. I think I have an idea what parents mean when they say they would rather take their child's illness for themselves. Still, Sammy had prepared me to focus on being grateful in all things. Most especially, I was grateful for my husband's support and our shared beliefs and grief. He was my rock when I crumbled, and at other times our roles reversed. I saw both his strength and his tender heart in a way that made me fall in love with him all over again. I now believe there is a collective power in prayer. I felt lifted, during some of the most trying aspects of the ordeal, by a peace that passes all understanding. The outpouring of support from family, friends, coworkers, veterinarians, and fellow iguana owners was overwhelming in the most positive way. I recall one message in particular: "If you bring love rather than discouragement to the moment, you will find the strength is there." This message helped me continue to stay strong in showing love to Sammy even though I was terrified and heartbroken watching her decline. I learned how much love there is, and I knew that Sammy in her weakened state was giving me this wonderful gift of allowing me to feel all that love. The last gift she gave us on this earth was showing us how much amazing love and support there is for us. This awareness has truly softened and opened my heart.

At what I later learned was the exact moment Sammy passed away, I read a friend's words of encouragement, "When our loved ones are sick, the most important thing we can do is ask God, their creator, to take care of them." As I prayed that God keep Sammy in His loving arms, she left this earth on 8/13/13, less than two months away from her 12th birthday. On that same day, a painting (which I had purchased as a gift for a family member) arrived: Jesus holding someone entering the gates of heaven. I set the art in front of Sammy's enclosure along with her turtle buddy and the cards from the many lives she had touched. For such a non-vocal creature, her absence makes the house remarkably silent. I sob into turtle buddy and recall how in the past when I have cried like this, she has tilted her head and given me an attentive look with wise eyes that speak volumes. I think about how I told my sick Sammy to hang onto Jesus shortly before she passed. I recognize the grace with which she left us, so that we did not have to make that decision. She even waited for the vet to come into the room so that he could see that she was making the choice to go, and that she was doing so peacefully. What a beautiful gracious spirit my green angel is.

Sammy remains my green angel. Shortly after she passed, I had a vivid dream that she had found her way home and was waiting for us in her enclosure. I later realized that she came to me in this dream to give me the opportunity to love and nurse her back to health, as was my heart's desire. In the dream, I gave her many baths, we fed her favorite foods, and she became very strong and even feisty. In the dream's final scene, I held my robust Samantha as she ate a swiss chard leaf given by Zak; she then moved as she had often done to signify that she wanted to be let down. The feisty image she left me with as if to say, "Let me go Mama. I am fine now. Let me go."

Sammy's love continues to be poured out upon all different kinds of creatures. Sammy's cat tree, window ledge, heating pad, staircases, and water dishes were given to a local animal rescue that helps many cats and some dogs. I could feel Sammy's tilted head smile down at me as I spoke with the founder, whose love and commitment to animals makes her spirit soar. On a flawlessly gorgeous Labor Day, Sammy's enclosures were given to young men involved with animal rescue who have a beautiful female boa with bright green colors and markings decidedly like those on Sammy's tail. Basically, "Sage" resembles Sammy without legs. My jaw dropped when I saw the picture. Papa Boa, a very ambitious young man who is a true advocate for wildlife conservation, seemed almost speechless in amazement; this was the very Cages by Design enclosure he had been saving for but could not afford. He was surprised that it was free, and I could almost see the explanation forming in his mind and in his heart as he heard about Sammy and saw her pictures. I later learned that Papa Boa excels in parkour, leaping over obstacles and scaling walls with grace much like our Samantha. Parkour is an activity that embraces new perspectives in order to see the potential for movement. It might also be described as the art of expression without limitations. As Sammy's outdoor enclosure was moved away, a gorgeous blue lizard ran across our deck.

At the excellent suggestion of a very good friend, we moved our sofa so we could sit where Sammy sat and see what she saw. The very first thing that I saw every morning with Sammy was her smiling head tilted over the side of her hammock looking at me. Now, as I sit in the sofa, I realize that she went to bed every night facing my direction. I realize that my ever-attentive iguana had often turned away from the more scenic outdoor view to watch us.

We know that Sammy continues to smile down on us, head tilted, with a mouth full of banana in a bright sunny sky, and we will hold her again someday. Even through my tears, I am quite certain that she is sitting on her creator's lap eating a ton of bananas, and He is wiping her face and laughing while He says, "Well done, my good and faithful servant Sammy. Well done."[44]

---

[44]   Matthew 25:23.

Appendix A

Twenty Five Reasons Why
I Love My Sammy

1. You are very curious; you appreciate the simple things in life and you have helped us do the same.
2. You are gentle; you do not have a mean bone in your body and you seldom get angry. Instead, you resolve any irritability with us by slowly placing your hand on top of ours (sometimes you leave your hand on top of ours for a long time). If only more people could resolve conflict in such a nonviolent and loving manner as you.
3. You are forgiving; you do not stay irritated even though we may have waited too long to get you your bigger room.
4. You have a great sense of humor; you play silly games and practical jokes on us, and you perform admirable gymnastic stunts, my silly Sammy. You help us remember the importance of playfulness.
5. You know when I am down or upset; you come hug me and kiss me and look at me with concern, my sweet Sammy.
6. You are smiley and bright green most all the time. You are just a joy to be around.
7. You are silent and have helped us appreciate the value of silence. You always tell us what you want and we are learning to hear you.

8. You have taught me so much about your fascinating species.
9. You are admirably stubborn; you never give up when you have your mind set on something (a wall, a treat, or an escape).
10. You are gorgeous. You are a truly beautiful creature inside and out.
11. You introduce yourself to newcomers cautiously at first, and then with a sudden leaping hug that is very endearing.
12. You are a smart cautious girl with whom others must earn their trust; with those you trust it feels as if you have given us the world.
13. You appreciate the niceties of life: a pillow, a hammock, and especially the sun.
14. Your eyes are sweet and innocent at times and mischievous at other times.
15. You are especially cute when you run, sleep, and eat your bananas and your green beans.
16. You spend a lot of time relaxing, and you encourage us to do the same.
17. You eat so healthy, and you encourage us to do the same.
18. You have the innocence of a baby with the wisdom of an old woman.
19. You like to sit and hang out with us and sometimes even sit on our laps.
20. You cling on to me when I have been gone a while in a heartwarming welcome home hug.
21. You protect me when I am napping alone by sitting on my chest and keeping watch.
22. We are meant to be together, my little green angel.
23. You help me remember what is important in life—love—as I slow down from my busy schedule to join you in your lazy lizard luxury.
24. You are so strong: a tough little girl who has survived so much.
25. You are patient, kind, and gentle: what's not to love?

Appendix B

Caring For Sammy

Important Information:

Please call one of our cell phones with a daily update.

Phone Numbers:

Emily's parents

Zak's parents

Sammy's vet

Sammy's previous vet

Please remove shoes before entering Sammy's mansion.

Please make sure that the black sensor remains secured behind her top rock ledge. This sensor tells the heat lamp to shut off once the temperature reaches 100 degrees F, so that Sammy does not overheat. Sammy will pant like a dog in the rare event that she begins to get too hot. If you see her doing this, spray her face and body with the water bottle that sits to the right of the cage on the table.

As a general rule, Sammy should not be out of her cage more than a few hours during the day. Those UV and heat lamps are important for her to soak up.

Sammy must always be in her cage with all the doors shut and the living room blinds shut (to avoid the risk of too much direct sunlight causing her to overheat) when we leave the house.

Morning: Bath and Breakfast

By 9 A.M. please give Sammy her bath. Sammy's heat and UV lamps should have automatically turned on at 6 A.M. on the weekdays, and 8 A.M on the weekends.

Preparing Food:

We wash and tear off pieces of leaves the size of Sammy's head. Leaves include collards, turnip greens, escarole, watercress, and dandelion greens (whatever we can find that is fresh, the more variety the better: see also the Green Iguana Society). Please make sure to remove the large stems from all of the leaves. After placing the leaves on her dish, douse water on top of the greens.

Next, we grind up her vegetables. For example, wash and break off the ends of several green beans and/or snap peas (you can find bags of these in the store when there are no fresh ones in season), and place these in the food processor. We also slice up a few pieces of parsnip and either sweet potato or squash (acorn or butternut) and add these pieces to the food processor. After the veggies are processed, we spread them on top of the salad. If needed, please sprinkle with warm water to moisten and raise the temperature of the food. It is important that Sammy be fed food that is at room temperature, as her body cannot digest cold food.

Please cover Sammy's salad with plastic wrap until you feed it to her after her bath.

Bathroom:

We fill the bathtub with warm water (not too hot), enough to cover Sam's shoulders (she likes to swim around in there and is a good swimmer). We carry Sammy upstairs and place her in the tub. You may find it helpful to carry her upstairs on her large stuffed turtle (a.k.a. turtle buddy) for ease of transport. Put some water on a couple of paper towels (on top of the toilet) in order to prepare them as her bottom wipes. Please make sure to wipe her bottom clean so that we don't have a poopy-butt lizard running around the house! Sammy usually swims back and forth with her head under water right before doing her business. Immediately when you see the business, scoop it out of the tub with the bucket (this prevents Sammy from swimming into it when you pull her out). Sometimes it is too messy to scoop; in that case, just get the baby out of the tub before she gets dirty! I find it easiest to lift her up out of the water by placing one hand under her chest, so that her hands rest on my hand, while I wipe her bottom and dry her tail with the paper towel in my other hand. If you want, you can use the towel on the back of the bathroom door; drape it over your chest and shoulder and let Sammy climb onto it while you wipe her. Sometimes it is easiest to wipe her after setting her back in her hammock (taking care to not let her dirty little butt rest on the hammock until fully cleaned with moistened paper towels).

If Sammy is taking a while to complete her business, or if she is trying to jump out of the tub, run the water in the sink or even in the bathtub. This usually stimulates her to go. Please keep placing her back in the tub if she jumps out. Sometimes I think she thinks this is a game of water sports. If she does not go after 45 minutes of being in warm water, then she does not have to go this morning. Please try again at your next visit in the early afternoon. Don't worry because we have learned that it is normal for adult iguanas, including Sammy, to sometimes (although only occasionally) go for one day without business. It is very rare for Sammy to skip a day.

Cleanup:

Sammy might be chilled after her bath, so we put her back in her cage after her bath. Alternatively, on a sunny day she can sit on her heating pad on the downstairs bedroom window sill (her favorite place). When her dewlap or body begins to feel cool, please place her back in her mansion. Please watch her like a toddler when she is loose, as she tends to chew on the carpet. If she picks up a strand of hair or any other foreign object, this is very dangerous. Even a strand of hair could get wrapped around her intestines! If you see hair in her mouth, please pull it out immediately. Please remove the solids from the tub with the bucket if you haven't already, and flush this down the toilet. Then flush the tub out with hot water and disinfect with the spray bottle of animal disinfectant. Please rinse the tub clean of all disinfectant before the next bath!

Breakfast:

We are trying to make Sammy forage for her food in order to increase her exercise; however, while we are away on vacation you may "spoil" her by doing the following. Bring Sammy's salad to her and hold it in front of her while she sits on her windowsill or in her mansion. It often takes a long time for her to begin to eat, so please be patient! There is no danger in Sammy overeating. We often hand feed her the first leaf or two so that she is aware that food is available. She doesn't see very well with those eyes on the side of her head, so sometimes gently touching her lip with a leaf can alert her to the presence of food. On rare occasions, we place a few small pieces of bread ("croutons") on the salad in order to stimulate her to eat. Then, please cover her salad with plastic wrap and put it back in the refrigerator. Her salad will need to be warmed back up later by letting it sit for a bit and running some warm water over it while the plastic is still on, kneading down to the plate with your fingers until it no longer feels cold.

Lunch:

Around noon, please play with Sam, and give her salad. She might also like pieces of green beans.

Dinner:

Around 5:00 P.M., please feed Sammy more salad, play with her, and give her treats. All of Sammy's lights should automatically shut off at 7:30 p.m.

More Salad:

Sammy may want some more salad. Hold the salad up to her while she sits on her ledge. If she wants to come out and play, then she can eat wherever she wants. Sometimes she needs to be hand fed a leaf or two first in order to get her attention that food is available. She might take a couple minutes to get into it, and she takes her time eating! If she doesn't eat, but then later bobs her head, it is probably because she is then ready to eat.

Playtime:

Sammy typically likes to play around 5 p.m. If Sammy wants to play, she will be sitting in her hammock facing out. She will either climb onto my shoulders when I open the door to her enclosure or she will welcome me picking her up. Sometimes Sam even jumps down to the floor of the cage to let us know she is ready to play. Her favorite place to play is in the downstairs bedroom. She might just want to hang out on the bed or on the windowsill for 20-30 minutes, or she may prefer to climb all over us. Some days she may not even want to play, so we just let her be. She is allowed to roam anywhere in the house (except the kitchen and bathrooms) just as long as you make sure that she doesn't climb onto something and injure herself. In the rare event that she crawls under a bed or couch, immediately get a dish with some small pieces of bread or banana pieces to lure her out.

Treats:

One of Sammy's favorite treats is figs. While we are on vacation, she can have two or three figs. Cut off the ends, cut them into quarters, place them on a Tupperware top, and soften them with water. Another treat is green beans. We wash four or five of these, discard the ends, and break the beans into pieces before hand-feeding these to her. You do have to be careful because Sammy gets really excited about her beans. Although the last thing she wants to do is hurt you, she may accidentally bite you if your finger is not far enough away from her face. If you hold your finger, or anything green or yellow, in front of her face she might try to eat it! One of Sammy's favorite games is "Raining Beans." We simply toss pieces of beans onto the living room carpet and let her eat them (this likely reinforces her carpet-eating habit, but at least she eats beans instead of my hair at these moments).

Note: Cut-up pieces of grapes or peaches (without too much skin) are good treats also. And, rarely, we do like to give Sam a half banana. Please cut it up in medium size pieces on a dish and sprinkle with water to encourage her to stay hydrated. This treat can be especially helpful if she hasn't been eating much because she misses her mama and papa. She will run across a room to get a banana.

Sammy's Personalities:

Rambunctious Reptile:

Despite the abundance of nutrition she receives, Sammy sometimes insists on eating the carpet. This is not allowed. She does not respond to verbal commands; however, so she simply needs to be gently picked up. Please look for hair hanging out of her mouth that she may have picked up, and gently pull it out. She may be hungry (even after treats), and so placing her in front of her salad again is often a good idea. Also, you can hold up a washed collard leaf or swiss-chard leaf and she seems to enjoy tearing into that.

Sammy loves to climb. On her more rambunctious days, she will jump on tables, attempt to fly into the television, and shimmy up the speakers. She could seriously hurt herself by knocking something on top of her or by trapping her tail in a tight space. She does not realize this, of course, she is innocently exploring and so she just needs to be picked up and moved to a safer location (like the tree, her cage, or our bedroom). We often play with her in the bedroom by standing in front of her and letting her climb onto our shoulders. She usually jumps off the bed onto us in an apparent attempt to "win" by landing on the nightstand (be careful she doesn't get onto the nightstand). She seems really happy when she does this.

If Sammy is getting into too much trouble it is o.k. to give her a "time out" in her cage. Please remember that when Sammy is being hyper, she is just playing, being a happy, healthy ig, and getting exercise. It would be unusual if she doesn't settle down within a couple hours if you play with her.

Sweet Sammy:

Sammy likes the window sills in the living room and downstairs bedroom. Make sure to roll the blinds up in order to prevent her from climbing them, and also to enable her to view the outside. Often times, Sammy will run right to the window and chill for a while. Other days, she is affectionate and likes to sit on our laps or shoulders. Still other days, she prefers to bask under her heat lamp and not explore the house much at all. She is very human-like in that she is in a different mood every day.

Glossary

Chicken of the trees. In some parts of Central America, iguanas are eaten and are thus referred to as "chicken of the trees."

Green glare. The intense stare of an iguana, usually suggestive of anger.

Head Bob IQ test. An assessment tool in progress, the need for which has become apparent after observing the many subtle variations in iguana head bobs that communicate a wide range of thoughts and feelings.

IEP. Usually referring to Individualized Education Plans for some children with special needs, IEP in this context refers to Sammy's Iguana Eating Plan.

Iggy back ride. An iguana ride on a human's back and shoulders.

Iguana Mama. A female human who adopts and cares for her iguana like a baby.

Iguana Papa. A male human who is an exceptional father to an iguana.

Ig-wipped. As defined by Carroll McNeill per Melissa Kaplan's website, "the state of being beaten into psychological submission by your devotion to their every whim."

MK diet. Melissa Kaplan's recipe for iguana salad (Kaplan 2013).

Samazing. Amazing Sammy.

Sambassador. Sammy the ambassador.

Sambunctious. Sammy the rambunctious reptile.

Sammy Saturday. A sunny warm Saturday in which Sammy's humans devote their attention entirely to Sammy's every whim. Variations include Sunny Sammy Second Salad Saturdays and Sundays, which refer to Sammy's tendency to eat more on such days.

Shed Head. Sammy's nickname at times when parts of her head begin to shed.

Snalt. An iguana "sneeze," which is the natural process by which iguanas eliminate salt.

Spoiled baby attitude. Sammy's tendency to refuse her usual food after being "spoiled" with treats. Sometimes accompanied by a swagger through her salad and a look of disgust.

Snout to Tail Length. The full length of an iguana.

Snout to Vent Length. The vent is the bottom of an iguana, and the purpose of this measurement is to illustrate the length of the iguana's body sans tail.

Turtle Buddy. Sammy's turtle stuffed animal that she frequently cuddles.

Wippisms. See also "Ig-wipped." Wippisms are specific examples of being Ig-wipped.

References

Cages by Design. 2013. Accessed July 24. http://www.cagesbydesign. com/.

Chapman, Gary D. 2010. *The Five Love Languages: The Secret to Love that Lasts*. Chicago, IL: Northfield Publishing.

Cicero, Marcus Tullius. 2008. *Collected Works of Marcus Tullius Cicero*. Charleston, South Carolina: BiblioLife.

Collective Soul. *The World I Know*. Miami: Criteria Studios, 1995. http:// www.collectivesoul.com

Daily Good: News that Inspires. 2013. Accessed July 24. http://www. dailygood.org.

Frye, Fredric L. 1995. *Iguana Iguana: Guide for successful captive care*. Malabar, FL: Krieger Publishing Company.

Gilligan, Carol. 1982. *In a different voice: Psychological theory and women's development*. Cambridge, MA: Harvard University Press.

Green Iguana Society. 2013. Accessed July 24. http://www.greenigsociety. org/.

Hatfield, James W. III. 1996. *Green Iguana: The ultimate owner's manual*. Portland, Oregon: Dunthorpe Press.

Hoerber, Robert G., general editor, and Horace D. Hummel, Walter R. Roehrs, and Dean O. Wenthe, associate editors. 1984. *Concordia self-study bible: New international version*. St. Louis, MO: Zondervan Publishing House.

Kabat-Zinn, John, and Thich Nhat Hanh. 1990. *Full Catastrophe Living: Using the wisdom of your body and mind to face stress, pain, and illness*. New York: Bantam Dell.

Kaplan, Melissa. 2013. "Herp Care Collection." Last modified January 13. http://www.anapsid.org.

Kaplan, Melissa. 2000. *Iguanas for Dummies*. New York: Hungry Minds Inc.

Lizard Cages. 2013. Last modified April. http://www.lizardcages.com.

Maslow, Abraham H. 1943. A Theory of Human Motivation. *Psychological Review 50*, 370-396.

McRobert, Scott P. 1999. "Cues affecting human recognition in a captive iguana." Paper presented at the 36th Annual Meeting of the Animal Behaviour Society, Lewisburg, PA.

Rath, Tom. 2007. *Strengths Finder*. New York: Gallup Press.

Saint-Exupery, Antoine, and Richard Howard. 1995. *The Little Prince*. Hertfordshire: Wordsworth Editions Limited.

The Rolling Stones. *Beast of Burden*. Paris: Pathe Marconi Studios, 1977. http://www.rollingstones.com/

Whitman, Walt. 1973. *Miracles: Walt Whitman's Beautiful Celebration of Life*. Kansas City, MO: Hallmark Cards.